The Teacher's Guide for Effective Classroom Management

The Teacher's Guide for Effective Classroom Management
A Trauma-Informed Approach
Third Edition

by

Tim Knoster, Ed.D.
Commonwealth University of Pennsylvania
Bloomsburg

and

Stephanie Gardner, Ph.D.
Commonwealth University of Pennsylvania
Bloomsburg

·P A U L ·H·
BROOKES
PUBLISHING CO ®

Baltimore • London • Sydney

Paul H. Brookes Publishing Co.
Post Office Box 10624
Baltimore, Maryland 21285-0624
USA
www.brookespublishing.com

"Paul H. Brookes Publishing Co." is a registered trademark of
Paul H. Brookes Publishing Co., Inc.

Typeset by Absolute Service, Inc., Towson, Maryland.
Manufactured in the United States of America by
Versa Press, Inc., East Peoria, Illinois.

The information provided in this book is in no way meant to substitute for a medical or mental health practitioner's advice or expert opinion. Readers should consult a health or mental health professional if they are interested in more information. This book is sold without warranties of any kind, express or implied, and the publisher and authors disclaim any liability, loss, or damage caused by the contents of this book.

The individuals described in this book are composites or real people whose situations are masked and are based on the authors' experiences. In all instances, names and identifying details have been changed to protect confidentiality.

Library of Congress Cataloging-in-Publication Data

Names: Knoster, Tim, 1956- author. | Gardner, Stephanie, author.
Title: The teacher's guide for effective classroom management : a trauma-informed approach / by
    Tim Knoster and Stephanie Gardner.
Description: Third edition. | Baltimore : Paul H. Brookes Publishing Co., Inc., 2024. | Includes
    bibliographical references and index.
Identifiers: LCCN 2024005080 (print) | LCCN 2024005081 (ebook) | ISBN 9781681256139
    (paperback) | ISBN 9781681257150 (epub) | ISBN 9781681257167 (pdf)
Subjects: LCSH: Classroom management. | Effective teaching. | BISAC: EDUCATION /
    Classroom Management | EDUCATION / Teaching / General Classification: LCC
    LB3013 .K63 2024 (print) | LCC LB3013 (ebook) | DDC 371.102/4--dc23/eng/20240208
LC record available at https://lccn.loc.gov/2024005080
LC ebook record available at https://lccn.loc.gov/2024005081

British Library Cataloguing in Publication data are available from the British Library.

2028   2027   2026   2025   2024

10   9   8   7   6   5   4   3   2   1

Contents

About the Online Companion Materials

Purchasers of this book may download, print, and/or photocopy the Resources for Continued Learning and appendices for professional and/or educational use.

To access the materials that come with this book:

1. Go to the Brookes Download Hub: http://downloads.brookespublishing.com

2. Register to create an account (or log in with an existing account).

3. Filter or search for the book title *The Teacher's Guide for Effective Classroom Management: A Trauma-Informed Approach, Third Edition.*

About the Authors

 **Tim Knoster, Ed.D.,** Professor at McDowell Institute, Commonwealth University of Pennsylvania, Bloomsburg Campus; Executive Director, Association for Positive Behavior Support

Dr. Tim Knoster is a professor in the College of Education and Human Studies at the McDowell Institute at Commonwealth University of Pennsylvania (Bloomsburg Campus). Dr. Knoster is also the Executive Director Emeritus of the Association for Positive Behavior Support (APBS). He has been a special education teacher, a director of student support services and special education, as well as a principal investigator and program evaluator on various state and federally funded projects focused on school-based behavioral health and interagency collaboration emphasizing promotion, prevention, and early intervention to address non-academic barriers to learning. The application of trauma-informed approaches reflecting positive behavior support in school, home, and community settings has served as a foundation throughout Dr. Knoster's career. In addition, he has directed statewide training and technical assistance projects that have supported schools to provide inclusive services and programs for students with complex needs, as well as for children and youth who have experienced trauma associated with neglect and abuse. Dr. Knoster has extensively published books and manuscripts, training materials, and other practitioner-oriented resources concerning the linkage among research, policy, and trauma-informed practice in multi-tiered systems of support and positive behavior support, school-based behavioral health, interagency collaboration that is child and family centered, and inclusive school reform. He has also served as an advisor on matters of policy and practice to agency directors, legal staff and court authorities, as well as elected officials. Dr. Knoster has acquired a national reputation for his ability to translate research into daily practice across school and community settings.

 **Stephanie Gardner, Ph.D.,** Associate Professor of Special Education, Commonwealth University of Pennsylvania, Bloomsburg Campus; At-Large Board Member, The Pennsylvania Association of Colleges and Teacher Educators (PAC-TE)

Dr. Stephanie Gardner is an associate professor in the College of Education and Human Studies at Commonwealth University of Pennsylvania (Bloomsburg Campus), where she serves as a faculty member in the Department of Exceptionality Programs' Special Education Program. She is also a certified QPR Institute instructor providing suicide prevention training through the McDowell Institute and serves as undergraduate program coordinator for the Social, Emotional, and Behavioral Wellness PDE Endorsement at Commonwealth University. Dr. Gardner currently teaches courses focused on positive behavior supports and supervises dual-certification student teachers. She has a rich research background including evidence-based practices for individuals with autism spectrum disorder, socio-sexuality education for individuals with intellectual disabilities, and in recent years, has worked on several projects and publications focused on training preservice teachers in trauma-informed practices as well as using multimedia technology to improve classroom management practices and self-reflection skills. Prior to transitioning into higher education, Dr. Gardner worked with some wonderful students in her roles as an elementary learning support teacher and middle school life skills teacher.

In addition to impacting her field through teaching and scholarship, Dr. Gardner values her active role in PAC-TE, currently serving her second term as an At-Large Board Member. Through her involvement in PAC-TE, she was appointed to serve on the Pennsylvania Department of Education's Committee on Education Talent Recruitment to address the teaching shortage and develop a new Career & Technical Education Pathway for Pennsylvania schools to help strengthen the future pipeline of secondary students pursuing careers in the education field. She has been awarded several McDowell Institute Faculty Fellowships and the Provost's Award for Excellence in Research/Scholarly Activity on her campus, as well as honored with a statewide recognition by PAC-TE for Teacher Educator of the Year in 2021.

Preface

The state of the social and emotional well-being of our youth has been an increasing concern across our schools for a number of years, giving rise to additional challenges. Even prior to the pandemic, in many ways, schools had already become de facto mental health providers for our nation's youth. Given this reality, coupled with anticipation of increased needs as we collectively recover from the pandemic, we feel that educators need practical guidance in trauma-informed practice. This need served as our primary catalyst for writing *The Teacher's Guide for Effective Classroom Management: A Trauma-Informed Approach*.

Our intention in writing this book is to provide our fellow teachers with not only a helpful, user-friendly resource to guide the establishment of a healthy classroom environment for student learning, but one that is sensitive to addressing the social, emotional, and behavioral needs of all students, including those whose lives have been impacted by trauma. A significant number of young children and adolescents experience traumatic events that can adversely impact their healthy growth and development. Traumatic events include a wide range of experiences that threaten personal well-being, injury, and even death. These may be anything from exposure to abuse or violence at home or in school to experiences associated with natural or human-made disasters to chemical imbalances and chronic illnesses. Prior to the pandemic, more than half of all school-age students reported experiencing at least one traumatic event before they became eligible for their driver's licenses (Copeland et al., 2018). Events experienced during the pandemic exacerbated this state of affairs for our youth.

One piece of encouraging news is that most young children and adolescents are either sufficiently resilient, or develop sufficient degrees of resiliency, to recover from difficult experiences largely because of the presence of caring adults in their lives. Resilient young children and adolescents may experience short-term distress as a result of a traumatic experience but are able to bounce back and return to their previous levels of functioning within a reasonable amount of time. However, for others, this is simply not the case. The degree of resiliency is directly related to the balance between the risk factors and the protective factors in that child's life. Examples of risk factors include a history of abuse or neglect, ongoing stress, chemical imbalance, and chronic illness. Protective factors include (but are not limited to) healthy practices, good self-esteem, consistent home/family routines, and feeling close to at least one other person. The lower and/or less significant the risk factors and the greater the depth and breadth of protective factors, the higher the likelihood of a given student's ability to bounce back or become sufficiently resilient. It is equally important to note that resiliency is dynamic in nature and can ebb and flow over the course of a lifetime.

So, what does this mean for educators working in schools? Specifically, what does being trauma-informed in the classroom really mean? And here's a related question: When supporting students who have experienced trauma, is it appropriate for a classroom teacher to manage the ebb and flow of classroom routines, including providing reinforcement for desired behavior and redirecting students when they engage in undesired behavior, or will the employment of the usual classroom management procedures retraumatize students? These represent just a few of the common questions emerging in our schools today, and the reason we have written this book is to answer them—to provide educators with practical, user-friendly guidance to inform daily instructional practices with the goal of enhancing the classroom learning environment for all students.

The chapters throughout this book will address these questions. However, the important takeaway at this juncture is that effective implementation of positive behavior supports reflecting social and emotional learning in the classroom serves as the foundation for trauma-informed practice in schools.

We believe you will find this book valuable whether you are an aspiring elementary, middle, or high school teacher or a veteran of more than 20 years in the classroom. You should find the strategies presented here useful regardless of a student's age, socioeconomic level, presence (or absence) of family and community support, or identified disabilities. Throughout our book, we use first-person language to provide an easy and relatable read. We want reading this book to be a meaningful, enjoyable, and impactful experience for you that is valuable in your future interactions with your students. The practices and approaches described in this book, although described in a conversational manner, reflect empirically supported practice.

At the conclusion of each chapter, you will find a reflective exercise to help you connect the content to your present knowledge base and consider potential applications in your classroom. We hope you will find these exercises meaningful in promoting more intentional trauma-informed approaches.

Although each chapter of this book can stand alone, we encourage you to examine the highlighted approaches as a whole because they are part of an overall picture of effective classroom management. In other words, the whole is worth more than the sum of its parts viewed in isolation from one another. In addition, it is unlikely that you will find any one aspect of preventive practice highlighted here to be, in and of itself, a panacea, magic bullet, or cure-all in terms of classroom management. Instead, when implemented in concert with one another, the principles and practices we describe will help you establish and/or maintain a safe and supportive learning environment viewed through a trauma-informed lens. They will help you create a healthy balance between prevention and early and efficient intervention as it pertains to student behavior in your classroom.

We frame the application of the practices described throughout this book within the framework of a multi-tiered system of support. Those practices also align well with schoolwide positive behavior interventions and supports. Many schools strive to incorporate proactive approaches to meeting the academic, social, emotional, and behavioral needs of their students within these two frameworks. The center of the learning process continues to be the classroom, and level of achievement continues to be directly related to the degree of healthy mentoring relationships established between classroom teachers and their students.

The primary focus in Chapters 1–3 is to provide a context for effective classroom management practices approached through a trauma-informed lens. After introducing the basics of trauma-informed approaches in Chapter 1, we get to the root of why students act the way that they do in Chapter 2. Chapter 3 explains what teachers can do to be more trauma-informed as they support students with significant social, emotional, and behavioral needs, and Chapter 4 describes how trauma can uniquely influence student behavior. Chapters 5–8 introduce a simple but powerful mnemonic, **REAP** (**R**apport building, **E**stablishing expectations reflecting social and emotional learning, **A**cknowledging desired behaviors, and **P**roviding increased opportunities for student engagement). By striving to implement and reflect on the effective practices included in REAP, we are confident you will be able to "reap" the benefits of establishing a supportive, engaging, and motivating classroom environment. Chapters 4–8 1) clearly describe the preventive feature, 2) help you see the interconnectedness of these preventive features to those highlighted in other chapters, and 3) provide you with some guidance in approaches you can use to establish these preventive features holistically within your respective classroom setting. Chapter 9 provides some additional universal classroom trauma-informed redirection procedures for implementation if/when student behavioral errors occur. When implemented consistently to complement your preventive approaches, these redirection strategies can be effective, and reinforce your clear expectations, and enhance your use of instructional time. Chapters 10 and 11 build on the preceding chapters and further contextualize trauma, and trauma-informed care/approaches, within the bigger picture of children's mental health in our schools today. In these chapters, we provide insight into how the practices highlighted in this book are situated within youth suicide prevention to support the overall well-being of students. Within these final chapters, we provide easily understandable practices that you can use if a particular student (or small group of students) fails to respond sufficiently to your use of the preventive practices presented in Chapters 1–9. To help you make practical applications in your classroom and school, Chapter 11 helps address the question, "So, what else can I do, and how do these trauma-informed practices align with multi-tiered systems of support?" Last, we encourage you to spend time in our final section, Closing Thoughts on Self-Care, to learn some ways to boost your own resilience.

We are grateful that you are taking the time to read this book, and we are grateful for the opportunity to support your efforts in further becoming a champion educator. We fully anticipate that you will be able to pull valuable nuggets out of this resource to assist you in refining or transforming your own classroom management practices in order to foster a safe and supportive learning environment for your students. We sincerely hope that you enjoy REAPing the benefits of implementing the strategies shared in this book as you continue to grow as an educator in supporting your students.

Introduction

In these contemporary times, more people in our society are becoming increasingly open about discussing their social and emotional well-being, mental health challenges, and associated personal life experiences. One outgrowth of more open personal discourse is that, to varying degrees, individuals are increasingly willing to share the journeys that they and their families have navigated over time. In addition, with the rise in social media usage and related virtual platforms of expression, increasing numbers of individuals are becoming comfortable with openly sharing their stories not only in their immediate circle of friends but with a broader audience. In particular, there is much greater recognition today than in the past about the prevalence and impact of *adverse childhood experiences* (ACEs), traumatic events and the long-lasting effects that can emerge as a result of those experiences. Greater awareness resulting from outreach efforts promoted through deliberate messaging avenues (including Mental Health Awareness Month and aligned global and national campaigns to reduce stigma) has given rise to increased media attention. The increased visibility of these types of life experiences serves as the backdrop for this book and was, at least in part, our impetus for writing it.

We feel that it is important to share a few words concerning the nature of the content in this book before you begin reading the chapters. The topics of ACEs, trauma, and in particular suicidal ideation in youth can understandably feel emotionally heavy. For some readers, these themes may simply raise concerns and lead to additional follow-up questions. For others, these topics may trigger a strong visceral reaction and may even give rise to some degree of emotional distress. With this in mind, we felt it important to acknowledge the range of emotions that may emerge and the variety of reactions that you may experience. To be clear, we still want you to read this book. Our goal is simply to provide you with some foreshadowing so that you may support yourself proactively through your own practices of self-care.

Speaking of self-care, at the end of this book we have provided a few closing thoughts about the importance of self-care, including links to a number of excellent resources that many educators have found helpful over the years. Should you experience emotional distress as you work your way through the following chapters, we encourage you to reach out to a trusted confidant and take advantage of your local resources.

To give you a head start, the following are a few national resources that may be helpful to you:

- Dial 988 to connect with the National Suicide Prevention Hotline.
- Text 741-741 to access the Crisis Text Line.

As you work your way through the chapters of our book, we wish you well. Remember: the final section of the book offers our closing thoughts on self-care along with additional resources.

1

What Exactly Is a Trauma-Informed Approach?

If you are reading this book, you likely have a passion for teaching and a deep-rooted interest in meeting the needs of your students. You should find this content especially helpful if you work directly (or aspire to work directly) with young children or adolescents in a classroom setting. Most of us have experienced—or know someone who has experienced—the roller coaster of extreme highs and lows that a ride as a classroom teacher can send us on during a typical school year, let alone teaching during or in the aftermath of a pandemic. The amount of multitasking required of teachers can be mind-boggling. A teacher is truly a "jack-of-all-trades," wearing many hats to ensure not only their students' academic growth but also their social, physical, and emotional well-being.

Day after day, educators across the country work tirelessly to give their all to their students, putting into action Rita Pierson's statement: "Every child deserves a champion—an adult who will never give up on them, who understands the power of connection and insists that they become the best that they can possibly be" (2013). Champion educators are resilient. Champion educators are empathetic and caring. Champion educators are problem solvers and team players. Champion educators also engage in ongoing professional development and self-care to help them rise to the many challenges of the job.

> "Every child deserves a champion—an adult who will never give up on them, who understands the power of connection and insists that they become the best that they can possibly be."—Rita Pierson

WHAT IS A TRAUMA-INFORMED APPROACH?

Each new academic year seems to present new challenges. Educators are continuously kept on their toes. You may have to learn new curricula just 1 week before (or sometimes a month into) the new school year, and exhibit flexibility in creating engaging lessons with technology integration requirements as more schools move to one-to-one technology, all while trying to keep up with the unique needs of a new classroom filled with eager faces waiting to see what this new school year has in store. Each year, the student population entering our classrooms becomes increasingly more diverse in terms of race, ethnicity, disability, socioeconomic level, family system, family dynamics, gender identity, and social/emotional needs. Research suggests that as many as one out of every three high school students will experience some sort of mental, emotional, or behavioral health challenge at a given point in their school career (Schaeffer, 2022). Given this reality, it is no secret that teachers play a significant and increasing role in addressing the mental health challenges of their students.

The challenge of teaching is complex. Educators are expected to effectively teach all students in the midst of education reform initiatives and high-stakes testing mandates connected to annual teacher evaluations, as well as the most recent shake-up in the history of our education system: COVID-19. The pandemic forced teachers to jump on the fast track in learning not only how to teach virtually, but also how to juggle multiple instructional formats simultaneously and effectively to meet the specific learning needs of their students. We had to find new ways to manage online and hybrid classroom spaces while continuing to strive to support students' social, emotional, and behavioral wellness regardless of where instruction occurred.

> The bottom line is that, outside of the family, teachers have historically been, and continue to be, the single most important external catalyst for student achievement of academic, social, emotional, and behavioral learning outcomes.

The bottom line is that, outside of the family, teachers have historically been, and continue to be, the single most important external catalyst for student achievement of academic, social, emotional, and behavioral learning outcomes. The significant influence that teachers have is, of course, part of a community effort involving many key players who shape the lives of students. However, when we examine the many external factors and resources that influence student learning, the quality of a student's teacher is the single most important factor (Hattie, 2015).

Along with the increase in attention to trauma-informed practices in our schools, there has been increased confusion in the field as to what a *trauma-informed approach* to managing the classroom means. As mentioned previously, teachers are not routinely trained in how to promote learning with students who have experienced stressful, potentially traumatic events or circumstances. The term *trauma* is used to describe an event, series of events, or set of circumstances that is experienced as physically or emotionally harmful or life threatening; overwhelms the ability to cope; and has lasting adverse effects on a person's mental, physical, social, emotional, or spiritual well-being. In such cases, there is increasing concern by many teachers about avoiding retraumatizing students. The increase in awareness and concern is a good thing. However, confusion comes into play, given many teachers' limited knowledge base regarding the following:

1. The basics of trauma

2. The prevalence of trauma among school-age youth

3. How the vast majority of students recovers from traumatic experiences and mental health challenges without developing mental disorders

4. How application of sound, preventive classroom management procedures can be, in fact, trauma informed

5. How implementation of trauma-informed (universal preventive) practices in the classroom serves as a protective factor to build student resiliency as well as to lower the risk of youth suicide

A *trauma-informed approach* is, by definition, informed by the knowledge and understanding of trauma and its far-reaching impact (Substance Abuse and Mental Health Services Administration [SAMHSA], 2014). It spans service delivery models and integrates knowledge developed through research and clinical practice with the voices of trauma survivors. Four key assumptions outlined by SAMHSA underlie any trauma-informed approach:

> A program, organization, or system that is trauma-informed realizes the widespread impact of trauma and understands potential paths for recovery; recognizes the signs and symptoms of trauma in clients, families, staff, and others involved with the system; responds by fully integrating knowledge about trauma into policies, procedures, and practices, and seeks to actively resist re-traumatization. (2014, p. 9)

HOW DOES A TRAUMA-INFORMED APPROACH DIFFER FROM TRAUMA-SPECIFIC SERVICES?

It is important to understand the relationship between being trauma informed in classroom practices and providing trauma-specific services. A trauma-informed approach can be implemented in any type of classroom setting with any and all students. It reflects practices that are different from, yet support, trauma-specific services. As noted previously, most youth who experience traumatic events during their school years are able to successfully navigate those experiences as a result of the protective factors present in their lives. However, there is a portion of students who will require additional, unique services and treatment to recover from those experiences.

The terms *trauma-informed approach* and *trauma-specific services* are sometimes (mistakenly) used interchangeably because both signify care for students who have been exposed to traumatic stress. There are a number of critical differences between these two forms of care:

- **Goal.** Trauma-specific services are designed to explicitly address the root causes of trauma along with trauma-related symptoms of individuals and groups of students; trauma-informed approaches reflect a generalizable approach that emphasizes prevention across an entire school, including individual classroom and nonclassroom settings.

- **Consumers.** Trauma-specific services tend to be clinical treatment interventions for specific students; trauma-informed approaches address the nature of the overall school and classroom culture by implementing practices that create supportive learning environments for all students.

- **Providers.** Trauma-informed approaches align well with state-of-the-art practices implemented by educators in school settings; trauma-specific services are typically provided by mental health clinicians rather than educators.

To paraphrase Hopper and colleagues (2010), a trauma-informed approach is a strengths-based approach grounded in an understanding of, and responsiveness to, the impact of trauma. It emphasizes physical, psychological, and emotional safety. A trauma-informed approach requires vigilance in anticipating and avoiding institutional processes and practices that are likely to retraumatize students who already have a history of trauma, such as aversive punitive disciplinary procedures. The core practices that support positive behavior and social and emotional learning in the classroom are by nature trauma-informed, as they help to create a safe, healthy classroom climate. It is encouraging that many classroom teachers, to varying degrees, intuitively implement some version of these types of proactive approaches. Specifically, the following foundational practices serve as the bedrock of trauma-informed practice in the classroom:

1. **Establish expectations.** Establish positively stated behavioral expectations reflecting social and emotional learning (SEL) skills together.

2. **Build rapport.** Stay close to students and build strong relationships during academic and non-academic opportunities.

3. **Deliver positive reinforcement.** Deliver positive reinforcement at high frequencies as students meet the established expectations in an active learning environment.

4. **Provide opportunities to respond.** Offer students many opportunities to engage authentically with the curriculum.

5. **Redirect undesired behavior.** If/when undesired behavior occurs, use redirection guided by the inherent principles of positive behavior support and delivered in a respectful instructional manner.

Implementation of these core practices is essential for any given classroom to operate well.

A trauma-informed approach in the classroom reflects six key principles highlighted by SAMHSA (2022), all of which are relevant across educational settings:

- Safety

- Trustworthiness and Transparency

- Peer Support

- Collaboration and Mutuality

- Empowerment-Voice-Choice

- Sensitivity of/Respect for Cultural-Historical-Gender Issues

Specifically, application of a research-validated array of practices to support positive behavior and SEL provides a firm foundation to address these principles in the classroom.

In summary, approaching classroom management through a trauma-informed approach strengthens your ability to fully support students entering your classroom with a wide range of experiences and needs. Grounding your interactions and instructional decision making in such a manner promotes safety, community, and equity, allowing your students to experience greater levels of academic and social success.

A trauma-informed approach also encourages you to consider more carefully the impact of your interactions and established classroom environment on students and provides you with the insight to take a step back and delve more deeply into what might be influencing students' actions in your classroom (particularly those that you might consider problematic). In Chapter 2, we will take a closer look into factors and experiences that can influence children's behavior because being aware of such factors can better help to ground you in your approach to implementing trauma-sensitive practices in your classroom.

REFLECTIVE EXERCISE

Consider your past exposure to training in and/or application of research-based classroom management practices. In what ways have these aligned with some of the underlying assumptions and core principles of trauma-informed approaches as introduced in this chapter? In considering potential gaps that might exist, what are some ways in which you could more clearly align your knowledge base and/or practices with a trauma-informed approach in meeting the needs of your students?

2

Why Do Kids Act the Way They Do?

Why do kids act the way that they do? Boy, if there was a short answer to that question, we would not only share it with you, but we would shout it from the rooftops! Such an insight could be applied to solve other contemporary problems of the day related to adult behavior across our nation and globally. We believe that the key to understanding or decoding student behavior lies, first and foremost, in understanding our actions and the nature of our own behavior.

HOW CAN UNDERSTANDING OUR OWN BEHAVIOR GIVE US INSIGHT INTO OUR STUDENTS?

In other words, thinking about our own needs and how those needs influence our actions can help us gain insight into student behavior. We refer to this as thinking in the first person about your own experiences in order to understand others. There are causal roots as to why we act as we do within and across situations. As a general rule, our behavior, as well as that of our students, is not random (even though it may appear so from time to time). The interactive effect of both nature (personal predispositions) and nurture (the things that happen to us or with us in our lives) influences how we act or react.

> The key to understanding or decoding student behavior lies, first and foremost, in understanding our actions and the nature of our own behavior.

A simple analogy can help clarify what we mean by this interactive effect. Think of a science experiment in which you take two sets of fluids and mix them together. There is HCl (hydrochloric acid) in one beaker, and H_2O (water) in a separate beaker. Each of these fluids, when isolated in separate beakers under stable conditions, is reasonably safe to handle. However, when you mix these fluids in a third beaker, place a cork on that beaker, and shake it vigorously, you will likely experience a volatile effect, such as an eruption or explosion (please do not try this at home). This is akin to what happens when various factors in our lives come together within the ebb and flow of our daily experiences. Our actions and reactions are directly related to interactive effects between what some would call nature and nurture. In other words, whether you experience extreme stress or feel relaxed and calm and then act one way or another is not based exclusively on any single factor. Both our feelings and our actions (behavior) are direct outgrowths of the interaction between nature and nurture. Say that you experience a day that starts out poorly when you leave for work and just seems to go downhill throughout the school day. On returning home that same evening, you are likely to find that you are not as resilient or nurturing toward others as you might be following a better day in the field.

Sometimes, those closest to you are the first to notice your "altered state"; if they mention it to you, it can be like throwing gasoline onto smoldering embers—combustible to say the least. It is not that you love those at home any less at that moment in time—it is quite the opposite. What you are likely looking for when you become stressed is the unconditional love and support you have come to expect from those closest to you. When you are feeling exhausted and overwhelmed, however, the smallest thing can set you off in an ugly way, making everyone involved feel unloved and underappreciated.

These personal reflections concerning the relationship between feelings and actions are equally relevant for each of your students. Whether they are experiencing emotional distress on a given day (and as a result appear distracted or off-task) or are feeling relaxed and calm (allowing them to remain focused and on-task within the classroom), the interactive relationship between feelings and actions/behaviors is always present.

Just to compound the confusing task of decoding behavior, some kids are less resilient and find it more difficult to handle things than others. For example, we are sure you have (at least) one kiddo who, regardless of the challenges they confront, much like a proverbial cat, always seems to land on their feet after they fall. Then, there is (you fill in the name here), who, despite all of your best intentions and good faith efforts to structure activities that will improve their success in the classroom, typically responds to situations as if someone were out to get them. You may in fact face these types of experiences with your colleagues as well, with some appearing more resilient from day to day than others. It seems that some people (both kids and adults) have more natural insulation to fend off adverse factors in their respective worlds than their peers.

So, given all this, is it simply the nature of some individuals to do better than others when under stress? Or is it an issue of nurture? Can we alter our situations and circumstances so that no one (student or colleague) is exposed to undue or unhealthy levels of stress? The reality of this complex issue is that it is both. Given that it is both nature and nurture, understanding how we as human beings respond to stress can be helpful to inform our thinking.

WHAT IS THE STRESS RESPONSE SYSTEM AND HOW DOES IT WORK?

Our brains have a built-in alarm system designed to detect a potential threat and help us respond quickly in order to keep us safe. This system is commonly referred to as the *stress response system (SRS)* (see Figure 2.1). There are three main parts of the brain that play roles in our responses to stress: the brainstem, the limbic system, and the neocortex.

The Stress Response System

1. The amygdala senses the threat and sets off an alarm.

2. The thinking brain assesses the situation.

3. The thinking brain goes offline. The "emotional brain" activates the fight-or-flight response.

4. The thinking brain helps shut off the alarm and helps us calm down.

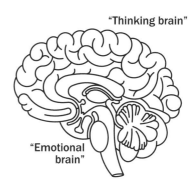

"Thinking brain"

"Emotional brain"

Figure 2.1. The stress response system. (Adapted from Guarino, K., & Chagnon, E. [2018]. *Trauma-sensitive schools training package.* National Center on Safe Supportive Learning Environments.)

The *brainstem,* located at the base of the brain, controls all of the major systems that keep us alive; it regulates our heart rate and breathing. The brainstem prepares our body to react when we experience a traumatic event. Think about how your heart races and your breathing quickens when you slam on the brakes to avoid an animal darting out into the road.

The *limbic system,* the emotional control center of the brain, determines how we feel about an experience (e.g., whether it is pleasurable or frightening) and helps us look out for danger and react accordingly. Within the limbic system, two structures play key roles in how we respond to stress. Much like a smoke detector, a structure called the *amygdala* helps us identify a potential threat, and it sounds an alarm of sorts when activated. The second structure, the *hypothalamus,* hears the alarm and communicates that message to the rest of our body to prepare us to respond. Think of the limbic system and the brainstem as your "emotional brain," sometimes referred to as the "downstairs brain."

The *neocortex,* commonly referred to as the "thinking brain" or the "upstairs brain," is the last part of the brain to develop. It helps us reason, plan, problem-solve, make meaning from our experiences, and regulate our emotions and behaviors. When faced with a threatening situation, our thinking brain assists us in deciding whether we are truly in danger and helps us return to a state of calm after the danger has passed.

Let's take a walk through the SRS, step by step, so you can see how it works:

Step 1. Your emotional brain senses a threat and sounds an alarm; this sends a message to your body to react. This happens at an automatic and unconscious level. For example, if you hear a loud noise, you jump immediately, before you are even aware you are in danger. Remember: When faced with a potential threat, you *react first* and *think second.*

Step 2. Your thinking brain assesses the situation to see whether the danger is real or just a false alarm.

Step 3. If your thinking brain perceives the threat as real, it temporarily goes "offline," and your emotional brain takes over and starts up your *fight-flight-or-freeze response* (often referred to more simply as the *fight-or-flight response*). During this time, hormones, including adrenaline and cortisol, are released to give your body the energy to fight or flee and to help you calm down once the threat has passed, similar to the gas pedal and brake pedal in a car. The types of physical changes your body experiences when the fight-or-flight response is activated include increased heart rate and blood pressure, rapid breathing, sweating, tunnel vision, and difficulty thinking clearly. When neither fighting nor fleeing is an option in the moment, your body may freeze (shut down).

Step 4. Once the threat has passed, your thinking brain helps shut off the alarm, putting the brakes on to allow your body to calm down and come back into balance.

> An experience becomes traumatic, or can lead to long-lasting effects, when it *overwhelms* the SRS.

Note that not every experience that sets off the SRS is traumatic. It is also important to understand that not every traumatic event results in long-lasting effects. An experience becomes traumatic, or can lead to long-lasting effects, when it *overwhelms* the SRS.

The risk for experiencing trauma increases as attempts to fight or flee are not effective in preventing or managing the perceived threat, making us feel increasingly helpless, vulnerable, and out of control. Think about pressing your foot on the gas pedal with the car stuck in neutral. The engine is revving at a high RPM, but you're going nowhere. Under these circumstances, your emotional brain continues to sound the alarm and send messages to fight or flee.

Over time, we can come to misread common everyday situations as threatening, triggering us and making it appear to others as if we are overreacting—or underreacting. Our SRS becomes so overstimulated and hypersensitive to perceived threats to our well-being that we start reading nonthreatening situations as dangerous, causing us to operate disproportionately in survival mode. Here is one example. Kenya experienced repeated physical abuse as a young child. As a result, Kenya's SRS was continuously overstimulated. When Kenya enters the kindergarten classroom and the teacher approaches to provide a pat on the shoulder paired with some praise (a typical form of positive interaction), Kenya reads this situation as threatening and recoils abruptly.

> Resiliency—our own as well as that of our students—is dynamic and can be further strengthened through positive experiences and by expanding the array of protective factors in our lives.

Resiliency—our own as well as that of our students—is dynamic and can be strengthened through positive experiences and by expanding the array of protective factors in our lives. What this means to us as educators is that what we do in the classroom, day in and day out, will have an impact, positive or negative, on the degree of resiliency of our students.

SO, IS IT NATURE OR NURTURE?

Reflecting on how the SRS works provides a useful frame of reference for thinking about why students act as they do and for understanding how each person's life experiences influence how they respond to various situations. Personal life experiences form a kind of narrative. Individual narratives vary, influencing how students might behave in different ways under seemingly similar circumstances. This is particularly important to consider when working with a student who has experienced—or is currently experiencing—trauma. The ways in which students experiencing trauma react are not static or hard-wired, with predetermined diminished outcomes. To the contrary, students can learn to navigate their life experiences, even those that have resulted in trauma, in ways that enhance their resiliency and success. However, different students are likely to require different types or degrees of support to have the opportunity to succeed in school.

Nature (i.e., biology or genetics) versus nurture (i.e., environment) is an age-old debate that has preoccupied many in the field. In reality, even though complex issues tend to be portrayed in simplistic sound bites in our society today, the important issues of life are rarely as clear-cut as asking the question "Is it X, or is it Y?"

> The important issues of life are rarely as clear-cut as asking the question "Is it X, or is it Y?"

In other words, both nature and nurture affect how we (as well as our students and colleagues) act at any given moment in time. How we act or react may change across situations or over time, so in the classroom our experiences from day to day can look as clear as mud. This daily soup we call life can become even harder to understand when we allow ourselves to get trapped into playing the unproductive either-or game of nature versus nurture.

WHAT IS THE A-B-C CHAIN?

So, how do you go about making sense of all this? Practically, what is a teacher supposed to do with all of this in the classroom? Well, the key is understanding two basic aspects of why kids act the way they do. First, all behavior (even behavior that appears challenging or perplexing) serves a purpose (technically referred to as a *function*). The behavior helps the student address an unmet need. In its simplest form, the actions of our students can best be viewed by looking for behavior patterns through an A-B-C chain of events:

- **A:** The *A* represents antecedents that set the stage for, or trigger, the behavioral response of the student. These antecedents (*triggers*) may be categorized into immediate/fast-acting antecedents (*fast triggers*) and slower-acting/slower-setting events (*slow triggers*). A few examples of potential triggers for students include feeling embarrassed in public, being angry toward another student without sufficient self-regulatory skills to manage that anger, and experiencing the pain associated with loneliness or isolation with limited access to (or opportunity to form) healthy relationships with others.

- **B:** The *B* part of the chain is the behavior of concern itself. A few examples include refusal to do work, off-task behavior (e.g., talking to peers when they should be working, doodling, daydreaming), or yelling at a classmate.

- **C:** The *C* represents the consequence(s) from engaging in the behavior of concern, or what actually happened following the behavior. The consequence helps identify the possible function of the behavior (e.g., escaping an unpleasant situation, gaining access to needed attention from others, feeling physically relieved from some form of pain they were experiencing).

The A-B-C chain does not legitimize problem behavior. Instead, it is simply a tool for decoding its causal factors. There are various levels at which behavior can be viewed. At the most basic level, it is helpful for us as educators to view the behavior of our students in the broadest sense through a trauma-informed lens. At the most complex level, individual intensive student-centered behavior support plans can be developed based on the results from functional behavioral assessments (FBAs). Such assessments should help to identify important information pertaining to immediate environment events in concert with insight concerning the individual student's life experiences and circumstances, as well as their hopes and aspirations.

Knowing that all behavior serves a purpose (function), it is also important to realize that behavior is context related, or situational. Acknowledging the importance of context is an important key in understanding why your kids act as they do across situations and in helping them grow and learn in your classroom.

Context encompasses not only the immediate environmental conditions or situations within the instructional setting, but also each learner's prior experiences—their personal narrative. This is particularly important to consider when working with a young child or adolescent who has experienced trauma, and it may help to provide insight as to why particular situations that appear innocuous to others trigger undesired reactions. When challenging behaviors are exhibited by our students, rather than asking, "What is wrong with you?" you can be more intentional in shifting your perspective to a trauma-informed lens by asking instead, "What has happened to you?" (Dorado et al., 2016; Wolpow et al., 2009). It is equally important to acknowledge what you cannot control (e.g., exposure to previous adverse childhood experiences [ACEs] outside the classroom, which can lead to toxic levels of stress and trauma) in order to invest your time and energy wisely on things you can influence directly inside the classroom (e.g., forming caring relationships with your students and implementing trauma-informed practices to enhance your classroom environment).

> Parents send the best kids that they have to school; they don't keep the "good" ones at home.

The reality is that you "inherit" the kids in your classroom at a given moment in time. Parents send the best kids they have to school; they don't keep the "good" ones at home. As such, your job becomes meeting your students where they are in order to help them grow and learn over time.

Understanding the nature of behavior and the importance of context can help you understand more effectively why your students act as they do. In real estate, it has been suggested that selling a home is all about "location, location, location." Understanding student behavior, in a parallel sense, is all about understanding *function in context*.

Understanding function in context is equally relevant to you and the other teachers within your school building as it is to your students. If you happen to be teaching in a school implementing the multi-tiered system of support (MTSS) known as the Positive Behavioral Interventions and Supports (PBIS) framework (U.S. Department of Education, OSEP, 2023), it is highly likely that you have talked explicitly with your colleagues about the value of understanding the function of student behavior in context. On the other hand, if you happen to be teaching in a more traditional school system that is not yet applying a multi-tiered approach, understanding student behavior in context may not

> Understanding student behavior is all about understanding *function in context*.

be as prominent in the ebb and flow of operations within your school. The importance of this orientation to decoding student behavior is no less important under these conditions. In the latter situation, you may need to carefully think through how you will incorporate this understanding not only in your actions within your classroom but also in your conversations with your colleagues to encourage other teachers in your school to embrace this same approach.

Always keep in mind that, as a teacher, you have a direct influence on the context for learning within your classroom. Although each student may respond differently at different times, and some may appear more or less resilient than others, your approach will facilitate your students' academic, social, emotional, and behavioral success. To quote Ginott,

> I have come to a frightening conclusion. I am the decisive element in the classroom. It is my personal approach that creates the climate. It is my daily mood that makes the weather. As a teacher, I possess tremendous power to make a child's life miserable or joyous. I can be a tool of torture or an instrument of inspiration. I can humiliate or humor, hurt or heal. In all situations it is my response that decides whether a crisis will be escalated or de-escalated, and a child humanized or de-humanized. (1972, pp. 15–16)

REFLECTIVE EXERCISE

For this reflective exercise, think about your experiences with your students, current or past. Try to identify a few examples of situations that triggered dramatically different types of reactions from different students who witnessed (or experienced) the same event. We have provided a couple of examples to get you started (see Figure 2.2).

Event witnessed or experienced	Student 1 reaction	Student 2 reaction
Example 1: Experiencing a significant change in the typical daily schedule	Once the change was announced and explained, the student moved forward in a successful manner throughout the school day.	Once the change was announced and explained, the student appeared distressed and experienced an unusual level of distress throughout the school day.
Example 2: Witnessing another student inadvertently bump into a classmate on the playground, causing the classmate to fall down.	The student went over to help the student up off the ground.	The student crouched down near the ground, covering their ears, and began to rock back and forth while crying.
Your turn 1:		
Your turn 2:		

Figure 2.2.   Reflective exercise on student reactions.

3

Becoming Trauma-Informed

To help you become trauma-informed as you manage your classroom, you first need to understand the basics of trauma and how we talk about it. Let's start with the basics of trauma and its effects on growth and development.

HOW DO WE RESPOND TO STRESS?

We all experience stress in our lives. Some stress is associated with positive events, such as buying a home or transitioning to a new job. Other stress has a less positive basis, such as the need to care for an ill family member or (perhaps more pertinent to your role as an educator) navigating among virtual, hybrid, and traditional face-to-face instruction delivery methods. Through their own personal lenses, students also experience varying degrees of stress. Stress is a natural part of life for all of us.

As described in Chapter 2, we navigate the stressors in our lives through our SRS. Taking another look at the SRS will set the stage for delving into trauma-informed classroom practices.

As you learned, our brains have a built-in alarm system that alerts us about threatening situations. This survival mechanism allows us to respond in a way that keeps us safe. The primary control hub of our brain that responds to a perceived threat, the *limbic system* and *brainstem,* is more commonly referred to collectively as the emotional control center of the brain or the "emotional brain."

Another area of the brain essential to daily functioning is the *neocortex,* more commonly referred to as the "thinking brain." Your emotional brain sets off a personal alarm when it senses a threat, which triggers your body to respond. When you encounter a situation that appears threatening, you generally respond or react first, and think last. Keep the sequence previously illustrated and summarized in Figure 2.1 in mind as you learn more about trauma-informed approaches.

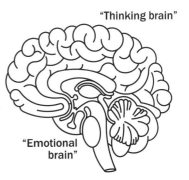

"Thinking brain"

"Emotional brain"

(*Source:* Guarino & Chagon [2018]).

When your emotional brain is triggered, you are less able to thoughtfully process information. It's as if your thinking brain has gone offline for a bit.

> When your emotional brain is triggered, you are less able to thoughtfully process information. It's as if your thinking brain has gone offline for a bit.

When you perceive a threat, your emotional brain engages in the *fight-flight-or-freeze response* of the SRS. This response occurs as a result of the release of the hormones adrenaline and cortisol, which provide your body with the energy it needs to respond. In this sense, your emotional brain helps you survive the immediate situation that is perceived as threatening. Once the threat is no longer present, your thinking brain comes back online to allow you to carry on with your typical daily functioning.

The SRS is truly an amazing, and useful, survival mechanism. However, for some of us, including students experiencing emotional distress, it can become overstimulated and subsequently dysregulated. *Dysregulation* simply means not functioning in a regular manner. When the SRS sounds the alarm too often or too intensively, it impairs the ability to self-regulate behavior. As challenging as this is for adults, it is even more challenging during the developmental years of childhood and adolescence and can have long-lasting detrimental effects. This has direct relevance to an understanding of trauma and trauma-informed approaches in the classroom. When stress levels reach unhealthy or, worse yet, toxic levels that overstimulate a child's SRS, trauma may be experienced.

WHAT IS TRAUMA?

Recall from Chapter 1 that the term *trauma* is used to describe an event, series of events, or set of circumstances that is experienced as physically or emotionally harmful or life-threatening, overwhelms the ability to cope, and has lasting adverse effects on a person's mental, physical, social, emotional, or spiritual well-being. The manner in which a traumatic event is experienced moving forward following that experience by an individual is related to their degree of resiliency, which is directly associated with the balance between risk and protective factors in their life. How any given student processes events that occur in their life is influenced by many things, not least of which are their prior experiences. Students who have been exposed to multiple traumatic events, have a past history of anxiety problems or depression, or have experienced ACEs, such as family adversity, tend to be at higher risk of experiencing dysregulation of the SRS. Dysregulation can appear in many ways. These include (but are not limited to) overreacting to common, regularly occurring classroom events (e.g., low levels of background noise associated with student voices) or underreacting to events that would typically elicit a strong reaction (e.g., being verbally accosted in conjunction with bullying behavior by a classmate). Students who experience SRS dysregulation are also at a greater risk for mental health challenges. In Chapter 10, we address trauma-informed approaches with students experiencing mental health challenges.

When stress levels reach unhealthy or, worse yet, toxic levels that overstimulate a child's SRS, trauma may be experienced.

HOW ARE TRAUMA, TRAUMATIC EVENTS, AND ADVERSE CHILDHOOD EXPERIENCES RELATED?

Let's provide some clarity as to the nature of trauma, traumatic event(s), and ACEs. Although these terms are related, they are sometimes (mistakenly) used interchangeably. A working definition of trauma appears in the previous section. Let's focus here on traumatic events and ACEs.

The National Institute of Mental Health (NIMH, 2023) defines a traumatic event as "a shocking, scary, or dangerous experience that can affect someone emotionally and physically." Experiences like natural disasters (e.g., hurricanes, earthquakes, floods), acts of violence (e.g., assault, abuse, terrorist attacks, mass shootings), as well as car crashes and other accidents are all examples of traumatic events. Exposure to traumatic events such as a societal-level pandemic or a more singular-focused event such as being bullied may lead to trauma for some youth. However, it is important to note that not every youth who has been exposed to traumatic events will experience trauma. We will delve more deeply into this shortly, but first let's talk about ACEs.

Adverse childhood experiences is a term coined by Vincent Felitti, Robert Anda, and their colleagues in their landmark study conducted from 1995 to 1997 (Felitti et al., 1998). Originally, ACEs were considered to be composed of seven categories of childhood adversities:

- Physical abuse

- Sexual abuse

- Emotional abuse

- Witnessing domestic abuse

- Living with someone who was mentally ill

- Living with someone who abused alcohol or drugs

- Incarceration of a member of the household

Researchers found that the more ACEs reported by adults, the worse their physical and mental health outcomes (e.g., the greater the incidence of heart disease, substance misuse, or depression). The term *ACEs* has since been expanded to include other types of childhood adversity. More recent studies of ACEs funded by the Centers for Disease Control and Prevention (CDC) include the additional categories of parental divorce or separation, and emotional and physical neglect (Lacey & Minnis, 2020). Other studies have expanded the list of ACEs even further to include economic hardship, homelessness, and experiencing or witnessing bullying, violence, or discrimination (The Research and Evaluation Group, 2013). No single list identifies all ACEs, but those that omit adversity related to social disadvantage are likely to overlook children in specific marginalized groups, who are disproportionately affected by ACEs.

It is important to understand that exposure to ACEs is not exclusive to any one particular physical location. ACEs can occur both at school and outside of school (in the home and community). As an educator, your ideal approach is to build protective factors of sufficient breadth and depth in your classroom to help prevent exposure to ACEs in the first place. However, in the event that exposure to ACEs, such as bullying outside of your classroom or home or community-based ACEs, does occur, a trusting relationship with at least one teacher such as yourself at school can help mitigate the effects of exposure.

HOW DOES ALL OF THIS RELATE TO TRAUMA-INFORMED PRACTICE IN THE CLASSROOM?

> The degree of resiliency of a given youth is directly related to the balance between risk and protective factors in that youth's life.

Following exposure to a traumatic event and the experience of short-term distress, most children and adolescents are resilient enough to return to their previous levels of functioning within a reasonable amount of time. This, of course, depends on the nature of the traumatic event and their degree of resiliency. The degree of resiliency of a given youth is directly related to the balance between risk and protective factors in that youth's life.

The lower the number of risk factors and the greater the depth and breadth of protective factors, the greater the likelihood of sufficient resilience to bounce back from a traumatic event. It may come as no surprise that youth who have risk factors such as exposure to multiple traumatic events or experiencing family adversity and other ACEs tend to be at higher risk of dysregulation of their SRS.

> Being trauma-informed in your classroom involves coupling prevention with mitigation (harm reduction).

In an ideal world, exposure of school-age youth to traumatic events and all forms of ACEs could be prevented completely, but reality suggests that this is unlikely. Prevention of exposure is ideal, but it is also important to have the ability to mitigate the effects should exposure occur. Being trauma-informed in your classroom involves coupling prevention with mitigation (harm reduction).

The key to building resiliency in your students so they can effectively navigate whatever life events occur ultimately relates to protective factors supporting them. A large proportion of the most important protective factors is based on a foundation of relationships (see Table 3.1).

As educators, we are in a prime position to become an important protective factor in the lives of our students. We are also positioned to help our students learn how to build protective factors in their own lives. This is relevant in working with all students, but it is perhaps most important in working with students who have experienced trauma and those who are viewed as members of marginalized groups within the school and local community.

> It is important to view trauma-informed approaches at school through an equity lens to ensure equal access and opportunity.

It is important to view trauma-informed approaches at school through an equity lens to ensure equal access and opportunity. This requires differentiating the strategies we employ to address different student needs.

It is likely that you already differentiate your instructional practices to varying degrees to address the academic readiness and skill levels of your students. What we suggest here is more targeted differentiation as it pertains to their social and emotional needs.

Table 3.1. Important protective factors

Feeling close to a caring adult (at least one—the more the better)

Having safe and predictable home/family/school routines

Feeling connected with and respected by others, resulting in a sense of belonging

Feeling a reasonable degree of control over your own life

Having parental/family/friend support

Feeling connected to the community

Being able to access constructive recreation

Having sufficient economic security to address basic needs

Engaging in healthy personal practices

Having a reasonably strong level of self-esteem

Having good problem-solving skills

Avoiding alcohol, tobacco, and other drugs

Practicing spirituality and mindfulness

In an effort to best support the needs of your students, we encourage you to organize your trauma-informed classroom practices within a multi-tiered framework.

All students benefit from core, universal trauma-informed preventive approaches in the classroom. However, based on their life experiences and needs, some will require additional targeted approaches or perhaps even individual intensive supports layered over those universal and targeted strategies. The general framework of this multi-tiered approach, called a *multi-tiered system of support* (MTSS), is depicted in Figure 3.1.

Although we do delve into targeted and individualized trauma-informed approaches in Chapter 10, the primary focus of this book is on universal trauma-informed

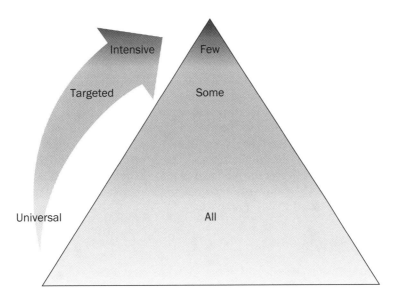

Figure 3.1. General framework of a multi-tiered system of support. (*Source:* Center on PBIS [Positive Behavioral Interventions & Supports], [n.d.].)

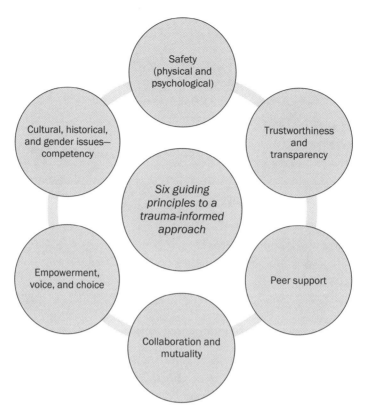

Figure 3.2. Substance Abuse and Mental Health Services Administration's six guiding principles to a trauma-informed approach. (*Source:* SAMHSA [2014].)

approaches within your classroom. The foundation of these universal strategies is the development of relationships and explicit instructional practices that reflect the six principles of trauma-informed care endorsed by SAMHSA (see Figure 3.2).

The following chapters address trauma-informed approaches to preventing undesired behavior (Chapter 4), developing rapport (Chapter 5), clarifying expectations reflecting social and emotional learning (SEL; Chapter 6), delivering high levels of positive reinforcement for prosocial behavior (Chapter 7), enhancing student engagement (Chapter 8), and redirecting undesired student behavior (Chapter 9). The universal strategies highlighted in Chapters 4–9 will support your efforts to build resiliency in your students in a trauma-informed manner that will enhance the learning environment for everyone, including you. Once you have absorbed these universal strategies, you will be ready for the final two chapters (Chapters 10 and 11), which hone in on meeting the needs of students experiencing mental health challenges and those with more complex needs in an equitable way.

REFLECTIVE EXERCISE

Alex, a 13-year-old middle school student, is becoming increasingly disconnected and disinterested at school. Alex fidgets, avoids eye contact, mumbles when responding to adults as well as classmates, and gives the impression of not caring too much about anything. Alex is close to grade-level capability of understanding course material and sometimes does well on assignments, but increasingly they refuse to engage with others during the school day. Many of Alex's teachers complain that Alex is "unmotivated" and has been shutting down during instruction (e.g., with head down and attempting to sleep during class). The teachers, who must keep prompting Alex to sit up and engage in the course materials, are becoming frustrated. Power struggles and disciplinary referrals are being reported. The power struggles frequently end with Alex either leaving the classroom or being sent to the office or guidance counselor.

Most staff at the school may not be aware that Alex has an extensive history of trauma and in second grade was removed from their home and placed with an aunt due to Alex's exposure to and firsthand experiences with severe abuse and neglect. Over the years, there have been several failed attempts at family reunification (particularly with Alex's mother, who continues to struggle with addiction).

Based on this scenario, please complete the final column in Figure 3.3.

Staff perspectives (without considering trauma)	Alex's perspective	Staff perspectives (with trauma glasses on)
Unmotivated; doesn't care	No one cares about me.	
Lazy	I must have done something wrong.	
Inattentive	I can't trust people.	
Noncompliant	I am worthless.	
Distracting; high maintenance	I feel hopeless.	
Disruptive to instruction	My teachers are mean to me. . . . They don't get it. . . .	
Distant; aloof	Why bother trying? . . . This situation is too far gone.	

Figure 3.3.   Reflective exercise on Alex's scenario. (*Source:* Guarino & Chagnon [2018].)

4

Preventing Undesired Behavior

Clearly, there is no magic wand you can wave that will make all undesired behavior disappear from your classroom. Each classroom has a diverse group of students with different strengths, needs, and interests, and who come from varying family systems, backgrounds, and communities. Then, there are the variables of the school setting itself: support personnel, available resources, curricula, extracurricular opportunities, and social networks. The reality is that you will never be able to prevent all undesired behavior from ever occurring in your classroom. However, based on how you interact with your students, you can have a strong positive influence that minimizes the incidence of such behavior. Establishing a few preventive trauma-informed operating procedures will enhance the learning environment in a way that can dramatically reduce the likelihood of nuisance and problem behaviors.

NUISANCE BEHAVIORS VERSUS PROBLEM BEHAVIORS

Nuisance behaviors are behaviors that, in and of themselves, are inconsequential. Examples include a student bouncing in their seat or calling out to get your attention once in a while rather than raising their hand. Inconsequential behaviors like these are best ignored. However, historically (or perhaps "hysterically"), nuisance behaviors have been known to elicit strong adverse reactions from teachers.

> You can have a strong positive influence. . . . by establishing a few preventive trauma-informed operating procedures . . . that can dramatically reduce the likelihood of nuisance and problem behaviors.

Problem behavior is behavior that can disrupt both the flow of instruction and the learning process, not only for the student exhibiting the behavior but potentially for their classroom peers. For example, a particular student who calls out consistently may result in others also starting to call out rather than raise their hands. Some problem behavior, such as verbal or physical aggression, can even create an unsafe learning environment. A student's problem behavior should be redirected immediately.

Perspective—your perspective, to be specific—comes into play in understanding that undesired behaviors are not always equal and knowing that, realistically, you will never be able to control all student behavior. This may seem like an odd statement in a book providing guidance on classroom management, but it is an important concept to understand; it can dramatically affect your perspective and subsequent approach to classroom management.

HOW DO WE MANAGE BEHAVIOR IN THE CLASSROOM?

One objection we have to the terms *behavior management* as well as *classroom management* is the potentially harmful implication of the word *management* in these common phrases. The very term implies a false notion of control, and it suggests that you are able to manage your students as if they were a group of programmable robots whose actions you can change with the flip of a switch. As enticing as this scenario may sound to some, it is not reality—nor should we want it to be. Instead, the goal should be to foster a nurturing and structured learning environment in which students feel valued and safe to express who they are while adhering to commonly accepted norms of behavior. This focus becomes even more imperative when working with students who exhibit concerning behaviors associated with traumatic experiences.

You can still provide support, even to those students who have experiences and circumstances that extend beyond your direct influence. How? It has to do with the way you structure your classroom and manage classroom interactions. Thankfully, these are practices that you can directly influence, which will help you have a purposeful, positive effect on your students' behavior. That said, the nature of these approaches has less to do with your students' behavior and more to do with your own behavior in the classroom. From our perspective, a more accurate descriptor than *behavior* or *classroom management* is "teacher self-management of instructional practice in group settings," but this term is far too long and will understandably not catch on in the field. So, we use the term *classroom management* for simplicity's sake, with the understanding that we are really talking about "teacher self-management of instructional practice in group settings."

> The goal should be to foster a nurturing and structured learning environment in which students feel valued and safe to express who they are while adhering to commonly accepted norms of behavior.

Starting off a new school year or taking on a new position naturally prompts you to begin planning your approach to classroom management. This often can appear to be a daunting task because there are so many variables to take into account for which to plan. On top of this, you have to think about differentiation, adaptations, and possible modifications to address unique student needs. The process of organizing the necessary resources to meet the unique needs of students can be greatly facilitated through schoolwide adoption of MTSS introduced in Chapter 3, along with PBIS. Regardless of whether your school is a PBIS school or a school with a more traditional approach to addressing student behavioral issues, the need to provide an array of classroom interventions and supports is present. So, there are various aspects to consider when designing a plan for your classroom, but ultimately it helps to keep things as simple as possible. After all, as a teacher, you have myriad responsibilities (e.g., grading, parent communication, curriculum planning, collaborative team memberships), so you want to make the best use of your time. Simplicity and efficiency are key.

PREVENTION VERSUS INTERVENTION

To keep things simple, let's break classroom management down into two main areas of focus: prevention and intervention. It is easy to become preoccupied with searching for an elusive answer to the question "What do I do when a student does X?" Although you will need a set of standard operating procedures to redirect undesired student behavior efficiently and safely, effective classroom management means reducing the likelihood that such behavior occurs in the first place. Think about it this way: A minimum of 80% of the time that you anticipate investing in managing student behavior in your classroom should be invested in preventive approaches. Being proactive in setting up your classroom management structure and approach should then result in having to redirect undesired student behaviors no more than 20% of the time. This so-called 80–20 split (80% prevention, 20% intervention) is generally accepted within the professional literature and is a common practice within effective classrooms. Broadly, this logic is used across the field and aligns with the three-tiered logic of the PBIS framework that invests in universal prevention first (OSEP, 2015). Precise tactics of teaching (or principles of practice) are relevant to both prevention and intervention, and they will help you achieve this 80%–20% balance.

WHAT IS REAP?

When used in tandem, four powerful preventive approaches will serve as a game changer in your classroom, whether you are teaching face-to-face or virtually. If you find yourself repeatedly telling your class to quiet down during transition times, struggling with students who seem unresponsive to your requests to answer questions when teaching, or noticing consistent disrespect for you and perhaps for peers, these proactive strategies can help you achieve improved classroom behavior. Each of these foundational practices, all grounded in research (Marzano & Marzano, 2003; Mitchell et al., 2017; Simonsen et al., 2008), is within your immediate influence as a classroom teacher. Regardless of the type of setting (elementary, secondary, general, or special education) in which you operate or the modality of instruction (face-to-face, virtual, or hybrid), the following principles of practice will allow you to "REAP" the benefits of investing more of your time in what matters most in your classroom (see Figure 4.1):

Rapport building

Establishing expectations reflecting social and emotional learning

Acknowledging desired behaviors

Providing increased opportunities for student engagement

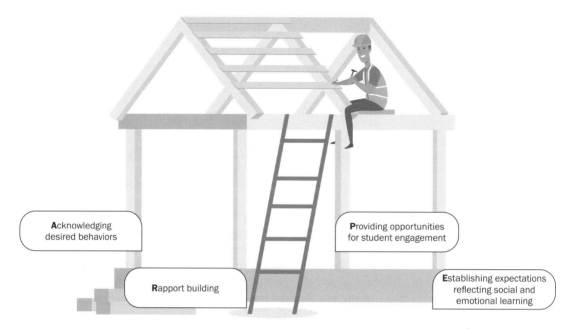

Figure 4.1.   REAP strategies for universal prevention. The four approaches are shown as the four cornerstones of the foundation of a house.

These four approaches, when viewed in concert, may best be visualized as the four cornerstones of the foundation of a house. Each component depends on the presence of the other three in order to bear the full weight of the house (student behavior in your classroom). When we get down to the root causes of undesired behavior(s), we can identify various underlying unmet needs (e.g., a need for attention, comfort in a predictable routine and structure, a desire to be engaged at a specific comfort level, a craving for positive feedback). Strategically planning your classroom management approach to reflect the REAP strategies can help you set the stage to provide the needed levels of support to all of your students.

The preventive practices reflected in REAP address SAMHSA's six core features of a trauma-informed approach introduced in Chapter 1. These core principles are depicted in Figure 4.2. SAMHSA's principles are informed by three areas: trauma-focused research, practice-generated knowledge about trauma-informed approaches, and lessons articulated by survivors of traumatic experiences.

Clinical interventions to support those experiencing the negative impacts of trauma have become integrated more widely into our behavioral health systems, but survivors of trauma have indicated that a reactive approach is not enough on its own (Magruder et al., 2016; SAMHSA, 2014). This is where other areas of our public sector are starting to step in to make their own services trauma-informed and more supportive to those experiencing trauma. School systems are one logical place in our society for an early and sustaining level of support to happen. We are already starting to see some of the adverse effects of the trauma that our children have endured throughout the pandemic, so schools should be front and center in implementing trauma-informed approaches with school-age youth. We provide a general overview of the various components of REAP here, and we delve deeper into each component in later chapters.

1. SAFETY   2. TRUSTWORTHINESS   3. PEER SUPPORT   4. COLLABORATION   5. EMPOWERMENT   6. CULTURAL, HISTORICAL,
                  & TRANSPARENCY   & MUTUALITY   VOICE & CHOICE   & GENDER ISSUES

Figure 4.2. SAMHSA's six core features of a trauma-informed approach. (From Centers for Disease Control and Prevention Office of Readiness and Response. [2020]. 6 guiding principles to a trauma-informed approach. https://www.cdc.gov/orr/infographics/6_principles_trauma_info.htm)

Rapport Building

The importance of establishing rapport with your students is (for the most part) a universally accepted understanding in schools today. Oddly enough, however, many teachers struggle every day to establish rapport with all their students, especially those who seem difficult to reach. In other words, we understand the importance of connecting with our students but are somewhat limited in our understanding of time-efficient systematic practices that make it possible. It is easy to establish rapport with students with whom you feel most comfortable. More often than not, these are the kids who provide you with a lot of reinforcement (e.g., are responsive to your instruction, follow directions the first time, provide you with positive feedback) and are the least likely to display undesired behaviors. You may even think of these kids as your "favorites." For the record, you are a person first and a professional second. You will have favorites. Acknowledging this reality is an important first step in establishing rapport with students who are more difficult to reach to ensure equity in your classroom approach.

You may find yourself gravitating toward your favorite students. This is just human nature. We would all rather hang out with others who make us feel good. The professional challenge is to 1) understand this aspect of our own human nature and 2) reach out and connect with those students who appear more distant or challenge our own personal comfort level. Having a few time-efficient rapport-building strategies in your teacher toolkit can help you establish a level of rapport with your most difficult-to-reach students.

When it comes to effective teaching, the bottom line is that most kids don't care what you know until they know that you really care about them (Albert, 1996). When students start to see your efforts to develop a relationship with them, they develop trust and feel safe, which can be very impactful for students who seem disconnected or feel vulnerable. Another bonus to purposeful rapport building with individual learners is that it positively impacts your entire classroom climate. It fosters more positive peer-to-peer interactions and collaboration, which again addresses some potentially unmet needs of students experiencing emotional distress that may be connected to trauma. Most teachers are nurturing, fun-loving, and approachable people but, for a number of reasons, not all their students may see them in this light (at least not right away). The rapport-building strategies described in Chapter 5 will help you reach out to, and connect with, all of the kids in your classroom.

> The bottom line is that most kids don't care what you know until they know that you really care about them (Albert, 1996).

Establishing Expectations Reflecting Social and Emotional Learning

Establishing a clear set of behavioral expectations goes a long way toward creating a classroom environment conducive to learning (and to developing rapport with each of your students). Behavioral expectations are essentially social norms. The rapport you build with your students becomes a by-product of your collective endeavors within the classroom. The teaching strategies you use to establish rapport are greatly enhanced when used in tandem with clear behavioral expectations that reflect SEL. Establishing (and teaching) clear and explicit performance expectations is a foundation in schools implementing the PBIS framework, so if you teach in a PBIS school, you are likely already familiar with this aspect of REAP. You have probably already experienced some degree of the positive effects of improved teacher–student interactions and relationships with your students (beyond simple reduction in undesired behavior). Establishing clear and precise behavioral expectations is equally relevant when teaching in a more traditional school setting. Establishing expectations is all about developing a set of norms within your classroom (whether it be in a brick-and-mortar building or on the Internet) that fosters social competence in all of your students. To be clear, this does not mean simply creating a list of "thou shalt" or "thou shalt not" rules. Rather, you need to identify three to five broad expectations (e.g., "be respectful," "be responsible," "be safe") and foster growth and progress toward them with each of your students on an ongoing basis.

Now, you may be thinking, "This is too simple. I mean, it can't be that simple, can it?" Although there are more operational details that you will need to address, starting at this basic level will steer you in the right direction. As the Roman philosopher Seneca noted, "If one does not know to which port one is sailing, no wind is favorable." You want to be sure that you are sailing in a direction with some promising landing sites ahead, instead of large icebergs to strike. Focusing your students' attention on what you want them to do (instead of what you don't want them to do) is one of the most important first steps you can take. Establishing clear expectations with your students adds transparency to your classroom structure and promotes a safe learning environment.

Defining three to five expectations across important settings (and routines) throughout your classroom day creates not only a road map for student behavior but also a radar system for you to use in reinforcing prosocial behavior. It also creates a healthy degree of predictability, and it helps your students realize that they have some power over their own success in your classroom (also known as *locus of control*). Students are empowered when they see that their voice was heard during the process of developing their classroom community. This applies to all students but especially those who have lived through trauma. Providing students who have lived

Focusing your students' attention on what you want them to do (instead of what you don't want them to do) is one of the most important first steps you can take.

through trauma with positive reinforcement and a predictable set of expectations supplies essential supports grounded in a trauma-informed approach. Steps and procedures to engage your students in the process of establishing behavioral expectations that reflect SEL are provided in Chapter 6.

Acknowledging Desired Behaviors

> Providing students who have lived through trauma with positive reinforcement and a predictable set of expectations supplies essential supports grounded in a trauma-informed approach.

Once expectations have been established, it is important to acknowledge desired behaviors. Acknowledging desired behaviors through reinforcement is the third cornerstone of REAP. The best way to help students develop appropriate behavior is by being clear on expected behavior. The best way to reinforce that behavior is, as the saying goes, to "catch them being good." This is by no means a novel concept (we never said we were going to share new, earth-shattering ideas with you). What we are here to do is help you develop a new perspective about classroom management that allows you to bring together (in full force) basic aspects of prevention that will help you increasingly become a more effective educator. As easy as this might sound, it can be very difficult to find the positive in a challenging situation. We all tend to focus, or even dwell, on the negatives. It is a lot of work to pull ourselves out of that space and move forward. Our own personal experiences can result in our own implicit biases that, when left unchecked, can inhibit our ability to seek out the "good" in any given student and prevent us from watching closely for that moment when that student is being successful. Sometimes, it just takes a shift in mind-set and narrowing of focus to find those perhaps subtle but powerful moments to reinforce. Chapter 7 guides you through this shift in mindset to help you broaden your scope and find those moments.

> Sometimes, it just takes a shift in mind-set and narrowing of focus to find those perhaps subtle but powerful moments to reinforce.

Providing Increased Opportunities for Student Engagement

Our fourth cornerstone is providing increased opportunities for student engagement, often referred to as *opportunities to respond* (OTRs). The more you engage your students through a variety of methods of instruction (the more and varied OTRs you provide), the more they will engage with the curriculum and the less time they will have to engage in undesired behavior. You can employ a vast array of strategies to elicit student responses. Oral, written, and action responses can be easily integrated during lessons (both face to face and virtual) to promote high levels of active engagement, maintain a brisk pace of instruction, and provide increased opportunities for feedback to students (Archer & Hughes, 2011). Higher levels of engagement and feedback can in turn enhance student motivation to participate and increase their overall involvement in the learning environment. Increasing OTRs is an essential component of the foundation of effective classroom management with a trauma-informed approach. Specific strategies for providing increased opportunities for student engagement are highlighted throughout Chapter 8.

HOW CAN I FORM GOOD HABITS?

Hopefully you are starting to see the pieces coming together, showing how this book will support your efforts to establish or enhance a solid foundation of prevention in your classroom. As Benjamin Franklin once said, "It is easier to prevent bad habits than to break them."

Each of us forms habits. Those habits, good or bad, develop over time depending on how they are reinforced. Whether the habit be kindness or rudeness, the principle of reinforcement (along with other factors) is always in play. Instructionally, your goal is to help your students develop habits consistent with the social competencies you have established with them in your classroom. Your students develop these positive habits as a direct result of your own development of positive teaching habits. The preventive approaches described here will help you to further develop those habits, and they will make reinforcing your students for engaging in prosocial behavior the norm in your classroom.

> As Benjamin Franklin once said, "It is easier to prevent bad habits than to break them."

It is important to understand that there are various forms of reinforcement. Not all reinforcement procedures—and most certainly not all potential reinforcers used by you as a teacher—will be equally powerful. Understanding the nature of positive and negative reinforcement and appreciating what is actually being reinforced is (much like interpreting a work of art) in the eyes of the beholder (the one being reinforced). Make no mistake: Both positive and negative reinforcement are intended to increase the likelihood of future recurrence of desired behavior. However, as you will see in Chapter 7, positive reinforcement is the goal you want to achieve.

Rapport building, establishing expectations reflecting SEL, acknowledging desired behaviors, and providing increased OTRs serve as the four cornerstones of preventive practices in the classroom. This is not to suggest that other teaching practices—such as active supervision of your students, conducting seamless transitions between activities in your classroom, or planning for more student choice to promote autonomy—are irrelevant. On the contrary, they are quite important. What we are suggesting is that these four practices are the primary foundation of effective trauma-informed classroom management. Each one is important in its own right, but these practices become even more powerful when implemented together. These preventive practices should prove helpful to you regardless of school setting. If you are teaching in a PBIS school, these proactive approaches are consistent with universal-level (Tier 1) approaches. They are equally applicable if you are teaching in a more traditional school setting. Each of the next four chapters describes one of these principles of practice and focuses on specific, related teaching strategies, but keep in mind that the whole is definitely greater than the sum of its parts.

REFLECTIVE EXERCISE

You are a second-year middle/secondary teacher in a high-poverty, diverse school district, which is quite different from where you grew up and also went to college. Many of the students in your class come from single-parent family homes (with a few parents currently incarcerated), and some are being raised by their grandparents. As you are being observed by your principal, you are trying to lead the class in a discussion about a text, but all you hear is silence. No one is volunteering to participate, and it is making you wish you had embedded more engaging teaching strategies prior to today's lesson to get students more comfortable with sharing out loud. Two of the students in your class have their heads on their desks, and when you try to call on one of them to participate, the student replies, "I don't know or really care right now."

Reflecting on the REAP prevention strategies just introduced, which of the cornerstones might you engage with and possibly seek out professional development on, knowing how critical they can be? Use Figure 4.3 to reflect.

REAP Prevention Strategies	Notes on Strategies to Reflect and Refine (Connecting to the previous above)
Rapport building	
Establishing expectations reflecting social and emotional learning	
Acknowledging desired behaviors	
Providing increased opportunities for student engagement	

Figure 4.3.   Reflective exercise on the REAP prevention strategies.

5

Building Rapport

As we move into this first cornerstone of REAP, think about some teachers with whom you have interacted in the past who stand out to you in terms of their connections with students—good or bad. Here are two notable individuals from our own personal experiences we would like to share with you.

- A particular high school teacher was simply brilliant in terms of his knowledge of the English language, breadth of understanding, and ability to describe in detail. Mr. Brice was incredibly gifted in the subject matter, and it was obvious that he was passionate about it. However, most of his students learned very quickly that Mr. Brice's passion clearly started and ended right there. He taught English to students rather than teaching students English. It seemed that just about every student struggled in Mr. Brice's class, even the students in the honors program. Regardless of Mr. Brice's natural talent in the English language, he clearly struggled with student language. He did not communicate any personal interest in a large portion of the students enrolled in his class (or at least appeared not to care to).

- Mr. Boyer, who instructed American History and World Cultures, was a really fun teacher. When he wasn't teaching, he was always hanging around with his students, joking around, asking how we were doing, and often going out of his way to help even when it meant taking some extra time outside the classroom. He was clearly a competent teacher, both in terms of his knowledge of the subject matter and his understanding of students. Amazingly, vivid memories of not only the course content of American History and World Cultures but also the activities that occurred during class time are easily recalled to this day. Mr. Boyer's approach to teaching was to make connections with his students as he taught the value of history and communicated the importance of gaining an understanding of other cultures.

We share these experiences to set the stage for helping you understand the importance of establishing rapport with your students. This chapter highlights some approaches to building relationships based on trust.

WHY IS BUILDING RAPPORT SO IMPORTANT?

We all live our lives in the first person, seeing things through our own eyes. A personal approach that is student centered (as opposed to subject centered) is a necessary first step in creating an effective trauma-informed learning environment in your classroom. As American philosopher Sidney Hook stated, "Everyone who remembers his own education remembers teachers, not methods and techniques. The teacher is the heart of the educational system" (1963).

> Your students are more likely to become increasingly motivated to learn and perform in your classroom if they understand that you have a genuine interest in them as people.

Regardless of prerequisite knowledge and/or interest in any given subject, your students are more likely to become increasingly motivated to learn and perform in your classroom if they understand that you have a genuine interest in them as people. This becomes even more crucial when supporting students who have had limited positive relationships or meaningful connections with others in the past and who may be yearning for someone to appreciate and to accept them for who they are as a person. Many students experiencing trauma can have difficulty not only in attempting to make sense of what they have experienced, but also in developing and sustaining relationships with others. Investing the time in showing your students that you care about them can have significant impacts on their emotional well-being and their engagement in school. This investment is also an important aspect of culturally responsive teaching, which fosters success and engagement for students from diverse backgrounds.

In many ways, creating a suitable level of rapport is a prerequisite for student achievement, especially for those who appear the most difficult to reach. Establishing rapport does not mean that you become each student's best friend. Gaining a closeness with your students positions you in their eyes as having their best interests at heart, even when what you are asking them to do at a particular point in time is not high on their priority list. Such relationships are based on trust. Trust, in turn, helps with student motivation, which requires thoughtful tilling and planting of the soil (as in a garden). Classroom soil that is conducive to student learning does not simply produce growth on its own. That growth is supported by your approach to teaching. Whether you are teaching in a school using a PBIS approach or in a more traditional school setting, and regardless of your modality of instruction, tilling this soil to build rapport is essential work.

> Establishing rapport does not mean that you become each student's best friend. Gaining a closeness with your students positions you in their eyes as having their best interests at heart.

This is true regardless of your modality of instruction. As we all discovered during the pandemic, there are many barriers to building rapport in a virtual and/or hybrid learning environment. Some learners participate from the comfort of their beds, others don't have a support system at home to encourage them to attend and stay focused, and some (both students and teachers) simply become burned out from sitting at a computer all day. Who didn't become "Zoomed out" from time to time throughout the pandemic? It takes creativity to build relationships with students virtually, but it can be done. Make no mistake about it, establishing rapport is a necessary building block for learning regardless of where the instruction is taking place.

HOW CAN I START BUILDING RAPPORT WITH MY STUDENTS?

Good question. How do you put in place the procedures that help you get and stay connected with your students? With many of your students, the process will be quite easy. However, with a few, it will likely require a more focused approach. What typically happens is that you will begin to develop rapport and a suitably close relationship with some of your kids sooner than with others. This will occur naturally and not particularly consciously on your part. Over time, you will become increasingly closer with a subset of your students to the degree that—if you're being honest—you might describe them as your "favorites."

As noted in Chapter 4, it is both natural and predictable to have favorites. This is not, however, the same as showing favoritism. The good news is that you will not need to spend much time systematically thinking about establishing rapport with these students because the relationships develop so naturally. It is your harder-to-reach students with whom you need to employ a systematic process to build rapport. These are the kids who do not, by their mere presence and actions in your classroom, provide you personally with the same degree of positive reinforcement as your favorites. To put it bluntly, it is these kids in particular whom you are paid to teach as a professional. If you are not conscious of your own personal biases, students who are challenging to teach may become "least favorites" or disciplinary "frequent fliers." In addition, students experiencing trauma may have built some unique walls as protective coping mechanisms that you will need to navigate around or over. So yes, problem solving is required to figure out how to establish a level of trust with these harder-to-reach students to light that spark of connection.

Your basic human instinct, almost an unconscious reaction, may be to minimize interactions with those students who do not provide you with a lot of positive reinforcement. The angst-ridden feelings in the pit of your stomach likely conjured by your more difficult-to-reach students will require increased focus on your own self-management skills so that you act in an equitable manner. Keep in mind that rapport is simply about building connection through trust with students, and a pathway of strategies that can assist you in that process does exist.

> Keep in mind that rapport is simply about building connection through trust with students, and a pathway of strategies that can assist you in that process does exist.

There are two primary considerations when consciously building rapport with a targeted student:

1. Determine the precise steps or actions (observable behaviors) involved in getting close with that student.

2. Apply rapport-building procedures in suitable situations.

Your use of these procedures is easily applicable in most educational settings. We also share some specific strategies for building rapport when interacting virtually. As with any other form of teaching activity, rapport building can be broken down into a series of steps. Using task analysis, the component steps can be viewed as links within an entire chain of events. During face-to-face interactions, consider the sequence of steps identified in Table 5.1 when systematically building rapport with your students.

These steps, originally outlined by Latham (1999) and expanded upon by us, may also be viewed as component parts of basic interpersonal communication skills. You can also use them as a form of curriculum with particular students who require help in acquiring basic social interaction skills.

As you consider these steps, you will likely envision ways in which to employ them during virtual interactions. Obviously, those that involve close physical proximity are not attainable, but others can be adjusted during virtual instruction. For example, in lieu of physical touches or gestures, you could send a virtual high five, a fist bump, or an emoji through the chat feature. Just as you would during in-person instruction, consider the age appropriateness and potential impact of your rapport-building efforts. Pace and colleagues (2020) shared some engaging ways to connect with middle school students during what they call "quaranteaching": having a virtual graffiti wall where students can share drawings, poems, or quotes in a public forum; creating a podcast or Voicethread about themselves to build classroom community; and tapping into familiar social media platforms. The use of nonverbal behaviors and body language can also be effective in an online environment. Simple actions can go a long way, such as ensuring that your full attention is on the students. Make sure your own cell phone is

Table 5.1. Steps in building rapport

✓ Demonstrate reasonably close proximity (generally within arm's reach).

✓ Demonstrate age-appropriate touch (e.g., fist bump, high five).

✓ Demonstrate appropriate facial expressions that reflect the nature of the situation.

✓ Demonstrate appropriate tone of voice that matches the situation.

✓ Demonstrate appropriate body language (e.g., appear relaxed, keep arms open as opposed to crossed, face the student, be attentive, look at student).

✓ Ask open-ended, positive questions (e.g., "What are you doing after school?" "How do you do so well in your track meets?" "What was your favorite part of the movie?"). If you ask questions that require one-word answers, that is what you will likely get from a student with whom you are not already close.

✓ Listen while the student is speaking. Ideally, talk less than the student (try not to interrupt or abruptly change the topic).

✓ Use empathy statements (e.g., "That sounds like an incredible experience. I'm so glad you were able to do that!" "I can't imagine how hard that was to say goodbye to your cat this weekend. I'm here if you need to talk more about it."). Act like a mirror and reflect the student's feelings by expressing your understanding and caring.

✓ Ignore nuisance behavior (if it arises) and let the little stuff (but not problem behavior) slide.

✓ Appear calm throughout the process, which can be easier said than done.

Source: Latham (1999).

silenced and out of reach; your camera quality, lighting, and background are good and nondistracting; and your facial expressions are positive when interacting with your students.

At first glance, understanding the mechanics of building rapport may appear relatively easy. However, don't worry if you feel nervous or anxious when applying these steps with a student (or small number of students) with whom you are already feeling distant. You are putting yourself out there and run the risk of being rejected in a nonverbal manner or on the bad end of a sarcastic comment. It is hard work to not take student actions or reactions to your attempts to reach out too personally and to really approach each attempt as a fresh opportunity.

> It is hard work to not take student actions or reactions to your attempts to reach out too personally and to really approach each attempt as a fresh opportunity.

It's not easy to "roll with the punches" when working to gain trust. Here's a story, shared by a teacher named Ms. Smith, about her interactions with one particular student, Marcos, a middle school student with a disability:

> The school year had already begun, and Marcos's family moved into our town from a neighboring district. Marcos had close friends and really liked his neighborhood in his old school. He was not happy . . . to say the least . . . about this change in his life. On top of the understandable angst most middle schoolers would have in this circumstance, Marcos was a student with mental health challenges and a survivor of trauma. The fact that I was one of the first faces Marcos saw on his first day in our building did not play in my favor, as he associated his disdain for this change in his life with me. Day after day, I worked hard to try to help Marcos feel welcome, safe, and comfortable in my classroom. Day after day, Marcos expressed contempt for being in our school and in my classroom, and toward me, despite my efforts. For instance, we were working in small groups on some transition-related skills where students were reflecting on career options and sharing in small groups. I was working with another group in the front of the classroom when I overheard Marcos share with his group that he wanted to be a mechanic, and then he added, "But if Ms. Smith ever brings her car to my shop, I will throw rocks at it and break her windshield." Needless to say, it took a lot of effort on my part to not take this comment personally, and I truly tried my best to start each day fresh with Marcos . . . working hard to provide him with positive feedback and getting to know his interests so I could incorporate those into my interactions with him. Now, I would be lying to you if I said magically my efforts quickly worked as if a switch flipped where we became best friends. However, I can definitely say that over time I earned his trust, and Marcos's negative actions and comments lessened to the point where I was even able to get a hug or two from him by the end of the year (which was a big deal in my book).

Having a clear understanding of these simple rapport-building steps can be reassuring when you begin to make your proverbial leap of faith toward particular students.

Now that you understand the basic mechanics of building rapport, you need to know the appropriate situations in which to employ them. Think back to some point when you were at a social gathering (e.g., a holiday party or just hanging out with friends). You know some, but not all, of the guests. Suddenly, you see a person you do not know but are attracted to in some way. If you are like most people, even though you may consider yourself courageous, you would probably not just take the risk and "go for it" by directly approaching that person. You would probably give some time and thought to a number of things before reaching out. Specifically, you might 1) think about how to approach them, 2) talk with someone at the event you already know who happens to know them, 3) think about what types of things might be of interest to them in order to start a conversation, and 4) find a natural (uncontrived) way to bump into them to get the conversation started. In other words, before you make your approach, a lot probably goes through your mind (even if it is within a very short period of time). You are concerned about meeting your soon-to-be acquaintance for a number of reasons, which can generally be summarized by the old saying, "You never get a second chance to make a first impression."

Now, with this mental construct in mind, think about a particular student (or two) with whom you need to develop a more conducive level of rapport. Give serious thought to their interests (e.g., music, sports, art). You may need to do a bit of reconnaissance by observing the student and their interactions with others, or by asking others who know them. Think about appropriate situations conducive to conversation in which you start a brief dialogue at some level regarding those interests. What we are talking about here can be described as "breaking the ice" with strategic use of "ice breakers." The key to starting the process of building rapport is to engage students in a conversation about their interests within a safe/targeted situation. It is important for your approach to appear natural and genuine, not rehearsed.

> What we are talking about here can be described as "breaking the ice" with strategic use of "ice breakers."

In terms of timing, look for brief periods of noninstructional time within the student's typical daily routine that would be conducive to social interaction (e.g., during homeroom or lunch, at transitions between classes or transitions within your classroom) so that your interactions do not depend on the student's success with an academic task. Look for small windows of opportunity—30 seconds here and 30 seconds there; making connections with a particular student is about small doses of highly frequent positive interactions over time. You want to provide free access to your attention (noncontingent on their performance and/or meeting expectations) in this sense.

How can you find such noninstructional times during the school day when teaching virtually? You can use the time when students sign on to Google Meet or Zoom early or stay online after class to engage in some conversation, have open office hours, create a student survey to solicit feedback to you on your interactions and teaching practices, or set up individual conference times. You can also send a personal message to a particular student via their LMS account to let them know you are thinking about them, offer an opportunity for academic support, or just share something about yourself. Some students might enjoy some company during the "down times" of their virtual day (during recess or possibly lunchtime) to chat or engage in a virtual game.

> Look for small windows of opportunity—30 seconds here and 30 seconds there; making connections with a particular student is about small doses of highly frequent positive interactions over time.

You can use rapport-building procedures in a number of ways, either in a one-to-one situation with a particular student or in small-group situations using other students (with whom your rapport is stable) as social brokers to the student of concern. There is no one right way to start the process. As you plan your approach, pick one that you feel the most comfortable with—or the least uncomfortable with—to increase the likelihood of more consistent use. As your confidence grows, you will likely find yourself using a combination of these approaches.

As an example, Jimmy is a student with whom you are having trouble connecting. After some investigative work, you have found out that he is really into video gaming and is a part of the video-gaming club at his middle school. You begin to look for short snippets of time during club time at school or during your common lunch period to ask his advice on video game purchases for the child of a friend. Over the course of a couple of weeks, you continue to build on these brief interactions by having additional brief conversations with Jimmy during transition times. After a month or so, Jimmy occasionally goes out of his way to find you to ask if your friend bought the games and if his kid liked them.

Understand that a student with whom you are trying to connect will unlikely open up to you after your first attempt to break the ice. Sometimes this does happen, but that is more of an exception. It is more likely that incrementally, over time, the student will gradually allow you to get closer to them as their comfort level with you grows. Like most relationships, the student–teacher relationship takes time to evolve, requiring patience and persistence on your part. To paraphrase John Quincy Adams, patience and perseverance have a magical effect that makes difficulties disappear and obstacles vanish.

> It is more likely that incrementally, over time, the student will gradually allow you to get closer to them as their comfort level with you grows.

The key to using rapport-building procedures is to use them whenever and wherever you find (or can create) the opportunity. You may need to create opportunities systematically with some students. Although the length of time this will take with any given student is unpredictable, you can have confidence that the relationship will likely improve over time by using this approach if you are patient and persistent in your efforts.

Also, unlike the personal social interactions that we asked you to reflect on earlier, understand that your initial rapport-building interactions with any particular student should not require a great deal of time. Depending on the situation, rapport-building procedures applied in this fashion usually take as little as 15 seconds to 2 minutes. The key is finding easily accessible, noninstructional times throughout the typical school day. Be sure to pick the more obvious times (easy and frequently accessible moments, such as typical transitions) rather than identifying less frequently available situations or settings (e.g., after-school events). The key (or power) is in the cumulative effect of your repeated interactions with your students over time.

These repeated relationship-building interactions are all part of a trauma-informed approach to teaching. Chapter 4 described SAMHSA's six core features of a trauma-informed approach to care: 1) Safety; 2) Trustworthiness & Transparency; 3) Peer Support; 4) Collaboration & Mutuality; 5) Empowerment: Voice & Choice; and 6) Cultural, Historical, & Gender Issues. In reviewing these principles, we hope this chapter has made clear a natural alignment with this first preventative approach to classroom management, which is truly

> Rapport building establishes trust. Trust lends itself to fostering a safe, positive, and respectful learning environment in which students feel valued and empowered.

grounded in relationships and addressing the needs of your students. Rapport building establishes trust. Trust lends itself to fostering a safe, positive, and respectful learning environment in which students feel valued and empowered. Demonstration of a personal level of care and interest in your students leads to engagement in culturally responsive teaching practices that can support students from diverse backgrounds.

As important as rapport-building procedures are—and make no mistake about it, they are essential—they represent only one of the four foundations of effective classroom management. Building rapport with your students will get you far, but by itself it is insufficient in terms of classroom management. Strategies to connect with your students must be combined with establishing expectations that reflect SEL—the second foundational strategy of effective classroom management within our REAP mnemonic—described in Chapter 6.

REFLECTIVE EXERCISE

Ryan is a fifth-grade student who moved into the school district about 2 months ago. After a brief "honeymoon" period of about 1 week, Ryan's academic and behavioral performance has been on the decline. Ryan also appears to be trying to enlist other classmates in a variety of undesired behaviors (e.g., asking you to repeat directions multiple times in a manner that appears, or at least feels to you to be, an effort to distract the class from progressing). When redirected, Ryan makes excuses, blames others, and verbally complains about you picking on him (e.g., "All you do is tell me I am messing up"; "You pick on me more than anyone else at this school!").

Reflecting on the importance of rapport building as addressed in this chapter, please complete the first two columns of Figure 5.1 to identify and plan some rapport-building strategies with Ryan.

Rapport-building strategies	When I could implement	Ryan's interests (possible connection points)
		Minecraft
		Mario Kart
		Laser tag
		Baseball

Figure 5.1.   Reflective exercise on rapport building with Ryan.

6

Establishing Expectations Reflecting Social and Emotional Learning

As we forge toward the future, it is helpful to be familiar with the past. Here's a quick glimpse in the rearview mirror, identifying the history of school discipline and, in particular, codes of conduct from the mid 1800s (see Table 6.1).

We find the behavior concerns (and corresponding consequences) from this era of whimsical interest. If "boys and girls playing together" was worth four lashes, what exactly did they have in mind in terms of "misbehaving girls" (10 lashes)? What if those girls were playing cards with boys while misbehaving around the creek, mill, or barn? Beyond the humor (and absurdity) of looking into the past, there is one important takeaway from our disciplinary history. The behaviors noted emphasize an exclusively punitive approach to establishing expectations about behavior. What is provided is simply a list of proverbial "thou shalt nots," with varying degrees of retribution. These are, of course, in keeping with the nature of the times, but it is interesting (and a little sad) that far too many classroom management approaches in schools today could be described as modern-day lists of "thou shalt nots." Consider the tone set in a classroom with the following posted rules:

1. Don't speak out of turn.

2. Don't take another person's belongings.

3. Refrain from using foul language.

4. No eating or drinking in class.

5. Do not get out of your seat without asking permission.

We hope that this exaggerated list gets our point across. The emphasis is on *what not to do* rather than on *what to do* (a more constructive approach).

Table 6.1. School discipline circa 1848 (a Selection of the *Rules of the Stokes County School*)

Offense	Punishment
Boys and girls playing together	4 lashes
Fighting at school	5 lashes
Playing cards at school	10 lashes
Climbing each foot over 3 feet up a tree	1 lash
Telling lies	7 lashes
Giving each other ill names	3 lashes
Swearing at school	8 lashes
Misbehaving girls	10 lashes
Drinking spirituous liquor at school	8 lashes
Boys going to girls' play places	3 lashes
Girls going to boys' play places	3 lashes
Coming to school with dirty face and hands	2 lashes
Calling each other liars	4 lashes

Source: Gatto, 2001.

HOW CAN I INFLUENCE STUDENT BEHAVIOR?

Both the literature and personal experience suggest that the most effective way to influence student behavior is by being clear about what you want your students to do, directly teaching the expected behavior, and then reinforcing your students when they do it. Although naturally occurring consequences for student misbehavior (short of the "lashes," of course) are certainly relevant, they are most effective when delivered in concert with high levels of positive reinforcement of expected behavior.

For example, we certainly do not want to see students bullying other students. However, the most effective way to minimize the likelihood of bullying behavior is not by punishment after it occurs, but by teaching and reinforcing prosocial skills (e.g., being respectful toward others) and providing a variety of clear examples. On the surface, this may seem like a matter of semantics, but in the larger scheme of classroom management, it is as different as sailing east compared to sailing west. We are not proposing that you take a utopian approach to classroom management in which life is beautiful all the time, there are no boundaries, and we all sit around giving group hugs. We all need to have specific procedures and consequences in place for undesired classroom behavior. This level of structure promotes clarity

> Both the literature and personal experience suggest that the most effective way to influence student behavior is by being clear about what you want your students to do, directly teaching the expected behavior, and then reinforcing your students when they do it.

and transparency in expectations. The key to reducing the likelihood of undesired behavior from occurring in the first place is threefold:

1. Establishing clear expectations for desired behaviors that reflect SEL.

2. Directly teaching the expected behaviors.

3. Reinforcing your students as they display those behaviors.

HOW DOES THIS CONNECT TO POSITIVE BEHAVIORAL INTERVENTIONS AND SUPPORTS?

Establishing expectations for student behavior in the classroom (and in schools in general) has received much attention over the years. Increasingly, schools have been expanding the application of scientifically validated approaches to enhance the academic, social, and emotional learning of students. A multi-tiered framework, PBIS, which is currently being implemented in thousands of schools across the United States and throughout the world, is one such approach. There is no question that establishing clear expectations is one of the cornerstones in the foundation of schools implementing PBIS, as well as a best practice in the classroom management literature (Korpershoek et al., 2016; Marzano & Marzano, 2003). However, and not surprisingly, there continues to be discussion in the field about implementing expectations that make sense and are feasible in *any* classroom—whether in a PBIS school or a more traditional school setting. It is important to breathe life into anything suggested by the research literature in a way that is both useful and user friendly. Table 6.2 identifies the fundamental aspects of establishing clear behavioral expectations in the classroom so that your students increasingly demonstrate social competence. Social competence helps you set the stage for developing the academic competence of each of the students in your classroom.

> Providing clear expectations gives your students a road map of actions that will increase their likelihood of positive consequences and academic success in your classroom.

Table 6.2. Fundamental aspects of establishing clear behavioral expectations in the classroom

✓ Select three to five positively stated, broad behavioral expectations.

✓ Identify your highest priority settings and/or routines within which you anticipate the greatest likelihood of undesired student behavior.

✓ Operationally define each of your three to five expectations across each of your identified settings/routines by asking yourself, "What would my students look like and sound like if they were being successful?" Try to engage your students in the process and incorporate social and emotional learning within the operational definition.

✓ Post your behavioral expectations in a prominent place in your classroom.

✓ Provide initial instruction concerning your expectations at the start of the year and provide booster sessions periodically throughout the school year.

✓ Reinforce your students on a regular basis for desired prosocial behavior—"catch them being good."

✓ Have clear, systematic (and reasonable) consequences for undesired student behavior.

Providing clear expectations gives your students a road map of actions that will increase their likelihood of positive consequences and academic success in your classroom. This level of predictability enhances transparency (with *trustworthiness* as well as *safety,* two of SAMHSA's six core features of a trauma-informed approach—see Chapter 4) and can provide a needed level of support for your more vulnerable students, including those experiencing difficulties associated with trauma.

Establishing and reinforcing clear expectations fosters a trauma-informed approach while also supporting *culturally relevant and sustaining educational* (CR-SE) practices. CR-SE approaches are inclusively minded and asset focused to support the needs of diverse—and typically underserved—populations of students (Johnston et al., 2017). This approach challenges us to examine our own potential biases, which can lead to misinterpretations of behaviors. Employing a strengths-based approach also aligns with establishing clear expectations and can help students to become even more empowered. An added bonus (and another best practice touched on later in this chapter) is offering students choices and a voice in the development of classroom expectations. This provides additional value by promoting community among all learners in your classroom.

SO, WHERE DO I START WHEN ESTABLISHING CLASSROOM EXPECTATIONS?

As the old saying goes, "You need to know the bull's-eye if you are to be held accountable for hitting the mark." Start by identifying three to five broad behavior expectations (no more than five, no less than three) that encompass the types of prosocial behaviors you wish to develop in your students (e.g., the "Three Bees": Be Responsible, Be Respectful, Be Ready; see Appendices A–C). There is no single set of expectations in the literature that can be applied to all classrooms; the key is to identify expectations that make sense to you and your students. Have fun with acronyms and mnemonics as appropriate. For example, some teachers have used the "Three Bees" and carried it through by employing a bumblebee theme in their classrooms throughout the year. Other sets of expectations include STARS (Strive to succeed, Try your best, Achieve to your potential, Respect yourself and others, and Safety first) and SOAR (Safe, Organized, Attentive, and Responsible). If you are teaching in a PBIS school, use the already-identified expectations that your school has targeted. If you are teaching in a more traditional school setting that has not adopted such a unified approach, you will, of course, have greater latitude in identifying your expectations.

Now that you have identified three to five broad, positively stated expectations, the next step is to think about the types of activities you will have the students do within your classroom. Think about both physical settings (locations) and routines that have historically produced the greatest likelihood of undesired student behavior. If you are teaching in a PBIS school, you may be able to draw from your school database (e.g., Schoolwide Information System [SWIS]). If not, rely on your intuitive recollection based on your instructional experiences. If you are new to the classroom, think about the types of situations that might be most likely to create undesired behavior or confusion (which can, in turn, generate undesired behavior). In other words, target situations/contexts that are most likely to give you the biggest headaches in terms of classroom management.

> Target situations/contexts that are most likely to give you the biggest headaches in terms of classroom management.

Specifically, think about how high-frequency routines associated with your expectations (e.g., entering and exiting the classroom, getting to work right away on independent or group work, asking for help when needed, sharing materials and supplies during group tasks) occur in physical locations within your room (e.g., coat/cubby area, supply areas, workstations, lab areas). If you are teaching in a virtual format, consider those virtual learning spaces or programs in which your students will engage most frequently when targeting your expectations (e.g., Google Meet classroom for direct instruction) along with instruction-associated routines (e.g., entering and exiting the virtual learning space, appropriate use of the chat feature during class, peer interactions in breakout rooms during unmonitored time, processes for asking or responding to questions in both synchronous and asynchronous situations).

WHAT IS SOCIAL AND EMOTIONAL LEARNING?

In addition to thinking through potentially problematic locations and routines, look to embed SEL within your respective classroom behavior matrix. The Collaborative for Academic, Social, and Emotional Learning (CASEL) provides evidence-based resources that emphasize consistency in expectations and practices to promote engaged learning and reduce conduct problems and anxiety (CASEL, n.d.; see Figure 6.1).

CASEL defines *social and emotional learning* as "the process through which all young people and adults acquire and apply the knowledge, skills, and attitudes to develop healthy identities, manage emotions and achieve personal and collective goals, feel and show empathy for others, establish and maintain supportive relationships, and make responsible and caring decisions" (CASEL, n.d.). Integrating SEL into your classroom expectations fosters social-emotional competence by teaching self-awareness, self-management, responsible decision making, relationship skills, and social awareness. It can also provide additional skill building for students exhibiting more challenging behaviors or those at risk with more targeted behavioral support (Mahoney et al., 2021). The following are some guiding discussion questions you can use with your students to help determine possible SEL connections (CASEL, n.d.):

- What type of school do you want to be a part of, and what would it look like and sound like?

- How should we talk to one another?

- How should we resolve a problem or a conflict?

This line of inquiry can be further focused on your individual classroom (CASEL, n.d.):

- What does it mean to have a classroom that feels "safe"?

- What are ways you can feel safe or unsafe both physically (in your body) or emotionally (in your feelings)?

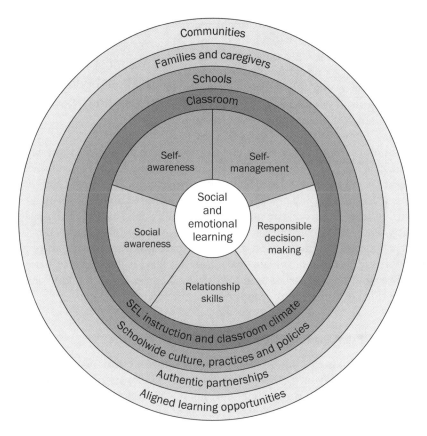

Figure 6.1.   Social and emotional learning (SEL) conceptual framework.
(From Collaborative for Academic, Social, and Emotional Learning. [2020, Oct.1]. CASEL's
SEL framework: What are the core competence areas and where are they promoted?
https://casel.org/casel-sel-framework-11-2020/; reprinted by permission.)

- Why is it important that we create a classroom where everyone feels safe and ready to learn?

- How do you want your classmates to treat you so you can feel safe?

- What are some ways we can agree to treat one another in our class?

Ultimately, by weaving some of these questions into your class discussion about expectations, you will be able to meaningfully engage your students and infuse important life-skills components into your behavior matrix. Think about how potentially empowering it could be for some of your students to be heard in this way. Having conversations with your students about their needs, safety, and feelings can be a game changer.

Once you have identified your three to five expectations along with your priority settings/routines, we encourage you to use the matrix found in Figure 6.2 (and included as a reproducible form in Appendix D) for planning purposes. After plugging your broad expectations into the left-hand side of the matrix and your priority settings/routines across the top, you are ready to take the next step in establishing your expectations for classroom behavior.

Expectations	Context 1	Context 2	Context 3	Context 4
Expectation 1				
Expectation 2				
Expectation 3				
Expectation 4				
Expectation 5				

Figure 6.2. Expectations planning matrix.

WHY ARE OPERATIONAL DEFINITIONS IMPORTANT?

The next step is to create an operational definition of each expectation across each targeted (priority) setting/routine. The most important reason for this is that desired behavior may look or sound different from setting to setting or routine to routine. For example, being responsible while doing independent seat work (e.g., taking a test) looks and sounds different from being responsible while doing group work. A simple way to think about operationally defining any given expectation is to ask yourself, "What would my students look like and sound like if they were meeting this expectation within this setting/routine?"

> A simple way to think about operationally defining any given expectation is to ask yourself, "What would my students look like and sound like if they were meeting this expectation within this setting/routine?"

Asking this question significantly increases the likelihood of creating operational definitions of desirable behaviors as opposed to creating a modern-day version of "thou shalt nots." To help you out, we encourage you to apply what has been commonly referred to as the "dead person test" to any behavior expectation that you establish in your classroom. Once you have defined an expectation within each setting/routine, ask yourself, "Could a dead person perform this expectation as stated?" If you answer "yes" (e.g., a dead person excels at "no pushing or shoving others"), then go back to the drawing board—your behavioral expectation is in need of revision. Applying the "dead person test" can help you minimize the likelihood of defining your broad expectations in terms of modern-day "thou shalt not" statements like those in the example at the beginning of this chapter. It can also help decrease the incidence of awkward moments with that one kid who always seems to be able to find the gray space in lists of rules by saying, "That wasn't on the list of things we couldn't do."

As you develop your behavior matrix, consider how you can move beyond the practice of emphasizing "compliance" (also known as "keeping a lid on it so the teacher can teach") in defining expectations by including a healthy balance of socially responsible behaviors. Being intentional about embedding SEL components in your behavior matrix can ultimately promote good citizenship as well as richer learning

Table 6.3. Traditional expectations complemented by associated social and emotional learning (SEL) skills

Context	"Traditional" expectation (implying compliance)	SEL-focused expectation
Be Responsible	Everyone does their fair share in group work.	Collaborate with team members and encourage others to share their perspective.
	Follow directions the first time.	Use my calming strategies (e.g., deep breathing) and let the teacher know if I feel confused as to what to do next.
	Complete work on time.	Encourage others; tell a peer they did a good job completing work on time.
Be Safe	Keep hands and feet to self.	I tell an adult when I am worried about my safety or the safety of a friend.
	Use walking feet in the hallway.	Hold the door open for others while walking in the hallway.
	Stay seated during lunch.	Choose a quiet or social area to sit in, and invite someone to join you during lunch.
Be Respectful	One person speaks at a time.	Encourage others to participate by listening quietly when they speak.
	Use appropriate language.	Speak to others in ways that build them up and make them feel good. Use positive self-talk as well.
	Only post relevant comments in the chat on Zoom.	Consider the feelings of others before I post a message. Reread my message before I hit send or post.

> By affording students the opportunity to participate in this process in a meaningful way, their voices can be heard as well as "seen" in the posted expectations.

experiences for your students. Some states may even provide guidance to educators on how to align SEL components, such as Pennsylvania's Career Ready Skills Continuum (Pennsylvania Department of Education, n.d.). In fostering SEL skills, you can set the stage for embracing and respecting diversity, which can result in more authentic student engagement. Table 6.3 provides some insight on how to complement traditional, or compliance-based, behavioral expectations with those that foster critical SEL skills.

Good instructional practices engage students actively as learners in the classroom, so it is important to engage your students actively in the process of defining your expectations across settings/routines. There are many good reasons to consider doing this; the two most important are as follows:

1. You are preteaching the expectations as a result of the process of asking the kids to help you define them.

2. You increase the initial degree of "buy-in" (motivation) because students have more ownership when helping you define the expectations.

Both of these reasons align directly with our emphasis on grounding classroom management practices in a trauma-informed approach that authentically engages students. By affording students the opportunity to participate in this process in a meaningful way, their voices can be heard as well as "seen" in the posted expectations. This level of engagement can help improve their sense of belonging, enhance the cultural responsiveness of the established expectations, and increase the likelihood of student success.

HOW CAN I INVOLVE MY STUDENTS IN THIS PROCESS?

Student involvement in this process can take many forms. The key is to find the form with which you are most comfortable. For example, at the beginning of the school year, you could have each student come up with some privately developed operational definitions and then have students do some pair-share work leading up to a large-group discussion in your classroom. You could also have students complete a Google Form survey on their thoughts, and then provide a later opportunity to analyze and synthesize the compiled data from the class in small groups. Or you could simply engage your students in a structured large-group discussion on the first day of school and (depending on the age and nature of your students) have them develop skits and/or demonstrations comparing appropriate and inappropriate classroom behaviors. Another creative approach used in some of the younger grades is for teachers to post photos of students in their class exhibiting desired behaviors as well as what "not to do" in targeted areas in the classroom; these are paired, of course, with written expectations prominently posted and (frequently) referenced in the classroom.

When teaching virtually, you can pair graphic symbols with examples and post them to your virtual classroom space. You can even display them in your Bitmoji classroom or with your daily agenda as a constant visual reminder.

Obviously, your professional judgment will serve as your primary navigational device. You need to ensure that the expectations developed with your class are relevant, respectful of culture, realistic, and aligned with your priorities. The key is to engage your students and actually have fun based on the best way to approach this process in your particular classroom.

As with any aspect of effective teaching, it is important to couple clear expectations for student performance and behavior with reinforcement on an ongoing basis. Post your established expectations clearly (whether in a physical or virtual learning space) to encourage your students to act in a way that creates a culture of social competence within your classroom. Relatedly, use of precorrection procedures within instructional blocks throughout the day to increase student success in meeting the established expectations is highly encouraged. To illustrate briefly, at the onset of a given lesson you remind your students of the established behavioral expectations prior to engaging them in the planned learning activity. You can also, as preferred, proactively provide occasional reminders throughout the activity to further increase the likelihood of student success. This same approach is used in nonclassroom settings in a PBIS school (i.e., the three to five expectations should be displayed prominently in locations such as hallways, the cafeteria, and other common spaces). The public posting of the expectations in tandem with your direct instruction and reinforcement procedures will serve as a reminder to your students, promoting development of a culture of social competence in your classroom over time. Public posting will also serve as a visual reminder for you to "catch your kids being good," which leads to the next foundational practice of effective classroom management: acknowledging desired behaviors.

> Post your established expectations clearly to encourage your students to act in a way that creates a culture of social competence within your classroom.

REFLECTIVE EXERCISE

You are preparing your behavior matrix for your 10th-grade science classroom for the upcoming school year. As you begin your planning, you review the established expectations that you used the previous year. This year, you want to expand your focus beyond basic compliant behaviors—which are still important, of course—to include expectations for socially responsible behavior. Based on a review of your expectations from last year, you have targeted a few particular expectations that lend themselves to expansion.

Using what you have learned in this chapter about behavioral expectations, complete the final column in Figure 6.3. We have provided one example to get you started.

Prior expectation to be enhanced	Aligned SEL expectation
Be Safe Use your own materials. Pick up clutter from your work area before leaving.	*Example:* Ask politely before borrowing materials.
Be Respectful One person speaks at a time. Follow directions the first time.	
Be Responsible Raise your hand if you need help. Be on time for class.	

Figure 6.3.   Reflective exercise on behavioral expectations. (*Key:* SEL, social and emotional learning.)

7

Acknowledging Desired Behaviors

As Maag (2001) stated, "Students' behaviors become challenging when traditional approaches to manage them have failed" (p. 174). Traditional approaches to manage behaviors in the classroom have often reflected reactive punitive techniques, which may address a behavior quickly but do not often have lasting positive effects at correcting said behavior (Maag, 2001). Contrarily, proactively reinforcing desired behavior provides the most viable approach. So how should you acknowledge desired (prosocial) behaviors in your classroom? The answer is something called *reinforcement,* and more specifically *positive reinforcement.*

WHAT IS REINFORCEMENT?

Reinforcement occurs when a stimulus in the environment strengthens a response (behavior), increasing its likelihood of occurring in the future (Skinner, 1953). There are two types of reinforcement: positive and negative. Understanding the similarities and differences between positive and negative reinforcement will set the stage for effectively selecting and using reinforcers with students as a part of your classroom management system. To compare these two forms of reinforcement, it will be necessary to use some technical jargon for a bit, so please hang in there:

> Understanding the similarities and differences between positive and negative reinforcement will set the stage for effectively selecting and using reinforcers with students as a part of your classroom management system.

- *Positive reinforcement* is the presentation of a desired stimulus contingent on the performance of a desired behavior to increase the likelihood of future recurrence of that same behavior. Presuming that a student finds verbal praise desirable, one example of positive reinforcement could be verbally praising a student after they demonstrate an expected social skill (e.g., sharing classroom materials with a peer during a group activity).

- *Negative reinforcement* is the removal of an undesired stimulus on the performance of a desired behavior to increase the likelihood of future recurrence of that same behavior. Presuming that a student who is having problems during class transitions would prefer not to be escorted by the teacher, an example of negative reinforcement would be to stop escorting them once they show improved behavior. In this example, the removal of the escort is the negative reinforcement.

Here are two illustrations of the similarities and differences between positive and negative reinforcement:

Sam. One of the expectations established with Sam, an 11th-grade student, was constructive use of assigned study hall time at the end of the day (2 days per week) to begin completing homework. Historically, Sam had been inconsistent—at best—with homework completion. It might have been possible to require Sam to sit next to the teacher during study hall to get Sam to work on homework, but Sam would likely have viewed this as "nagging," setting the stage for negative reinforcement (allowing him to sit where he desired contingent on him doing his work). If this became the predominant pattern of teacher–student interaction with Sam, compliance may have been realized in the short run, but because it depended on seating arrangement through the form of negative reinforcement, this would not be likely to lead to a sustained change in behavior. This approach may have also undercut rapport over the long run, as Sam may come to view the teacher as a "nag" and someone to be avoided. Instead, the teacher implemented positive reinforcement procedures by coupling behavior-specific praise (provided privately) with periodic proactive prompts (short of the dreaded nagging). As a result, Sam increasingly began completing homework during study hall and gradually completed greater amounts of homework over time.

Paula. Paula was virtually teaching elementary emotional support in a high-need urban school district during the pandemic. Student attendance and engagement were a daily struggle. During typical class sessions, only about 25% of the students logged in on time. Among those who did log in, the lack of meaningful participation was disheartening. Understandably flustered, Paula was providing increasingly frequent redirections to the students to get them to attend to their lessons. During a peer-coaching debriefing session, Paula was provided with some positive and specific feedback strategies to use that aligned directly with expected behaviors for virtual lessons. Paula was guided to shift away from predominantly applying contingencies such as requiring students to stay after the virtual class session ended (setting the stage for removal of this contingency based on improvement: negative reinforcement) to providing behavior-specific praise. One example of this was when Michal (who found verbal praise reinforcing) muted himself without prompting, Paula immediately followed his unprompted muting with "Michal, great job muting yourself when you were done sharing" (positive reinforcement). Paula even developed a personal goal to not only incorporate more frequent behavior-specific praise but also to deepen personal engagement with her students and invest in rapport building to improve overall attendance and interaction. Paula's increased use of publicly delivered behavior-specific praise with those students that found this desirable (positive reinforcement) resulted in a noticeable improvement in student responsiveness. Over time, there was a significant increase in daily attendance and student progress within their virtual learning environment.

The bottom line in both of these examples is that positive reinforcement is the constructive way to go. Now, make no mistake about it, both positive and negative reinforcement procedures are just that: reinforcement. In other words, negative reinforcement is not punishment. Both forms of reinforcement increase the likelihood of desired behavior. However, positive reinforcement should be the primary reinforcement procedure employed in your classroom for a number of reasons. Most important, it increases the likelihood of desired behavior in a way that helps you further build and maintain rapport with your students.

The use of negative reinforcement on a regular basis (which can become a very slippery slope) can jeopardize your rapport in exchange for dull compliance in the short run (think about the previous examples). Used sparingly—and interspersed with a lot of positive reinforcement—negative reinforcement can be useful, but it should come with a warning label: Use with extreme caution. When you frame your classroom management approach through a trauma-informed lens, there are obvious benefits to providing frequent positive feedback to students, especially to those who are at risk for needing more intensive supports. Finding opportunities to "catch kids being good" (providing the needed level of positive reinforcement) becomes very helpful in increasing the likelihood of desired behaviors and enhancing rapport with your students.

Often, students with complex needs are among the least likely to receive positive accolades. They either fly under the radar through withdrawn behavior or are frequent fliers in terms of receiving reprimands and consequences for undesired behaviors. Structuring moments to provide positive reinforcement for desired behaviors can take some extra attention and planning. However, it pays off over the long run in terms of your students' emotional well-being and engagement, as well as ultimately in their social and academic success.

> Positive reinforcement should be the primary reinforcement procedure employed in your classroom for a number of reasons. Most important, it increases the likelihood of desired behavior in a way that helps you further build and maintain rapport with your students.

> Structuring moments to provide positive reinforcement for desired behaviors can take some extra attention and planning. However, it pays off over the long run in terms of your students' emotional well-being and engagement, as well as ultimately in their social and academic success.

HOW DO I SELECT POSITIVE REINFORCERS?

So, now that you know that positive reinforcement is the name of the classroom management game, it is important to identify reinforcers such as praise, tangibles, activities, privileges, and attention that your students enjoy. Right away, consider the reinforcing nature of your time and attention, because these are readily at your disposal. We are not suggesting that attention is a universal reinforcer that will work with each student in all situations. Instead, attention is one of your most easily accessible reinforcers and (perhaps) the most powerful one. As French poet and Nobel Prize winner Anatole France said, "Nine tenths of education is encouragement."

The key to selecting reinforcers is figuring out your students' interests. Some kids respond well to public praise for performance. Others respond well to private praise and may respond even better to a combination of the two. The challenge is to understand your students and figure out what makes each one of them tick (so to speak). Acknowledging appropriate behavior in the form of praise is a relatively cost-effective form of reinforcement that you can use easily in your classroom. The power of praise can be maximized by following some simple tips:

- Use praise genuinely and deliver it contingent on student behavior. More simply stated, provide behavior-specific praise right after a student displays a desired behavior. If you praise just to praise, it will likely lose its effect.

- Be cognizant of your body language when delivering praise, and make sure your tone, demeanor, stance, and facial expression match your delivery of praise statements. For example, saying "Nice job helping your team to clean up your workspace, Aaron" in a flat tone without making eye contact with Aaron, while looking down at your desk grading papers, may not be as reinforcing as it could be when delivered in a genuine, upbeat manner that shows you are giving Aaron your full attention.

- Vary your praise statements over time. Using a praise statement such as "Kiss your brain for solving that problem," "Raise the roof for sharing your snack with Casey," or "Awesome-sauce—you were so thoughtful to help Ian clean up" might not be your cup of tea, but we are sure you can select a variety of behavior-specific praise statements that are within your comfort zone to add a little spice to your repertoire.

> Behavior-specific praise provides students specific, positive verbal feedback indicating approval of social or academic behavior, and when used effectively, it can improve your classroom climate (Cook et al., 2017).

Behavior-specific praise provides students specific, positive verbal feedback indicating approval of social or academic behavior, and when used effectively, it can improve your classroom climate (Cook et al., 2017).

To illustrate behavior-specific praise, consider the following example. Sean, a student in your kindergarten classroom, invites Erik to play a game of tag with a group of friends. Erik has had social difficulties in the past and has increasingly been self-isolating during recess. You watch as Erik hesitates but then with some additional prompting from Sean agrees to join the game. After recess, as Sean passes you to walk inside the classroom, you could say privately, "Sean, you are so nice." This statement could be motivating to Sean, but without explicit connection to the behavior, it may have limited effectiveness. Instead, for a long-lasting impact, you could provide behavior-specific praise, such as the following: "Sean, it was so kind of you to invite Erik to play tag. You are great at helping others feel welcome. I am proud of you." Providing precise praise statements best ensures similar desired behavior in the future. This level of acknowledgment, clarity, and detail is yet another clear example of a trauma-informed approach in your classroom.

Additional forms of classroom reinforcement include the use of tangible slips of paper or coupons in the form of a token economy, as well as earning points on a classroom reinforcement platform such as ClassDojo. ClassDojo is a platform on which school communities can set up spaces for schoolwide (think PBIS) or classroom-specific expectations to be virtually posted/accessible and student can in turn earn reinforcers throughout the school day from all school personnel they interact with (https://www.classdojo.com/). If you happen to be teaching in a PBIS school, the token economy or earning of points can easily be implemented in a way that is compatible with other lottery-type drawings already in operation. It is essential to pair behavior-specific praise with delivery of lottery-type tickets or other reinforcers regardless of whether you are teaching in a PBIS or more traditional school setting.

WHAT IS THE PREMACK PRINCIPLE?

One common reinforcement procedure involves applying the Premack Principle. According to the *Premack Principle,* access to something that is desired (a preferred stimulus) is made contingent on the performance or use of something less preferred by the student (a less-preferred stimulus) so that the likelihood of increased performance or use of the preferred stimulus becomes more predictable over time. In other words, a more probable activity can be used to reinforce a less probable activity. We hope we haven't lost you with these formal definitions of a well-known principle in the fields of psychology and education. A more user-friendly way to define this principle is to rename it the "Mealtime Rule" or "Grandma's Rule," familiar to parents and children alike: "You can have dessert after you eat all your vegetables." Think of it as a *first–then* or *if–then* statement.

Although important, the Premack Principle is nothing more than understanding that in life, sometimes you have to do one thing that you do not necessarily enjoy doing for its own sake (e.g., eating your vegetables) to gain access to another thing that you prefer (e.g., dessert). Some may say that this is nothing more than bribery or that it is manipulative. In a narrow sense, it is, but if this is true, then so too is much of life. Gaining access to things we prefer is often contingent on the performance of other things. For example, as much as we both enjoy teaching, we do get a paycheck every 2 weeks that we value highly. The reality is that the Premack Principle is in play every day in all of our lives. Table 7.1 provides additional examples of the Premack Principle in action.

> Although important, the Premack Principle is nothing more than understanding that in life, sometimes you have to do one thing... in order to gain access to another thing.

WHAT'S FAIR IS FAIR—OR IS IT?

Let's turn our attention to the pragmatics of providing reinforcement in your classroom. Here is one common misunderstanding about reinforcing student behavior: To be fair, everyone should get the same amount of reinforcement (e.g., number of instances of verbal praise, number of high-fives, the delivery of the same number of tokens). Fairness does not mean that everyone gets the same thing at the same time. Instead, fairness really means that each student gets what they need. Needs vary from student to student, and they change over time and across different situations. This understanding of fairness serves as the foundation for addressing issues of equity. To help you understand this point, here is a (paraphrased) illustration from Dr. Richard Lavoie (presenter at the 2004 F.A.T. [Frustration, Anxiety, and Tension] City workshop):

> You are attending a professional development training session at a local school when, suddenly, a teacher by the name of Susan slumps over in her chair, falls to the floor in full cardiac arrest, and appears to have stopped breathing. How ludicrous would it be if one of us said, "Susan, I would really like to help you out here. I mean, I know CPR and first aid. In fact, I am certified in both. I could save your life, but I just don't have time to give everyone in the classroom CPR. It just wouldn't be fair for me to give it to you and not to the rest of these nice folks in attendance here today. So although I don't like it any more than you do, I guess you are on your own." (Rosen & Lavoie, 2004)

Table 7.1. Examples of the Premack Principle in everyday life

Less-desired behavior	More-desired behavior
If you share your toys with others . . .	Then others will be more likely to share their toys with you.
If you appropriately say "please," "thank you," and "I am sorry" . . .	Then you will increase your number of friends in the classroom.
If you organize and complete your assigned work promptly . . .	Then you will earn higher grades and associated privileges.
If you consistently come home by curfew . . .	Then you can stay out until 11:00 p.m. on the weekend.
If you consistently drive responsibly . . .	Then you may have access to the family car when needed.
As a person in a relationship, if you will simply be still and listen (as opposed to trying to solve the problem) when your significant other is venting about something that upset them at work . . .	Then _____. (We are confident that you can fill in this blank.)
If you sit through watching *Frozen* for the 100th time with your kids . . .	Then you can soak up those sweet snuggles while you still can before they enter their teenage years and are "too cool" for that.

You see, the issue of fairness is really about equity by providing access to what students need so that those same students are in a position to benefit from instruction. This, in fact, is the underlying rationale behind sponsored endeavors, such as breakfast programs at school, free and reduced lunch endeavors, after-school child care, and other forms of extended school services. To reiterate, fairness really means that each student gets what they need with the understanding that personal needs will vary from student to student and that these needs can change over time and across different situations. Understanding fairness and equity in this way is an essential part of a trauma-informed approach to classroom management. This frame of mind definitely helps keep things in perspective when you are working hard to support students with more complex needs. It can help you address the "That's not fair to do—everybody deserves the same thing" naysayers with responses such as, "I am doing this for Keisha because it's the right thing to do, and it is exactly what she needs at this time."

This concept of fairness can help you differentiate your use of reinforcement to meet individual student needs. What is reinforcing to one student may not necessarily be reinforcing to another. Just because Kasey can't get enough of the *Baby Shark* song (and now it is likely stuck in your head as well—sorry about that!), it does not mean that the other 23 kiddos in your kindergarten class will be motivated to complete their writing assignment by the promise of watching a *Baby Shark* YouTube video when they are done. Sometimes, you may luck out and find a common reinforcer for a number of your students. However, this may not always be the case, especially when working in a more intensive manner with particular students with complex needs. Thinking about differentiating reinforcement can be very useful in two ways:

1. It helps you understand that what is reinforcing at a given moment in time is relative to the student being reinforced at that time.

2. It can be liberating (as a teacher) to understand that the goal is not to deliver the exact same type or amount of reinforcement (e.g., private verbal praise) from student to student as if you were a human candy dispenser.

It is important to understand the distinction between varying types of reinforcers and differentiating schedules of reinforcement. Both concepts will assist you with developing an individualized approach to reinforcing desired behavior. We already touched on the notion that what is reinforcing to one student may not be reinforcing to another. It is crucial to determine exactly what clicks for your students and to have a menu of options to increase student motivation and avoid satiation. In addition to varying the types of reinforcer(s) you provide (e.g., social, tangible, activity related), you will likely need to differentiate the schedule of reinforcement. This becomes even more essential when providing individualized behavior support as described in Chapter 11.

> It can be liberating (as a teacher) to understand that the goal is not to deliver the exact same type or amount of reinforcement (e.g., private verbal praise) from student to student as if you were a human candy dispenser.

HOW DO I FIGURE OUT THE RIGHT AMOUNT OF REINFORCEMENT TO PROVIDE TO MY STUDENTS?

There is no one answer to this question. There is not some preset number of times that reinforcement should be delivered on any given day. Instead, think about your reinforcement procedures as a proportion. For each instance of corrective feedback for undesired behavior, you want to provide (at least) four instances of positive reinforcement for desired behavior. This will help you achieve the often-noted 4:1 ratio in the education field (Loveless, 1996). When you achieve the 4:1 ratio, everyone gets access to the same thing. What differs, however, from student to student is the time interval within which the 4:1 ratio is achieved.

Let's say you have three kids in your first-grade classroom who are increasingly becoming distant from you (despite your best efforts to increase rapport-building opportunities). You find yourself correcting problem behavior with each of these three kids increasingly more often than with the rest of your class combined. On average, Zoe seems to warrant corrective feedback from you once a day, Darius about twice as often (once in the morning and once in the afternoon), and Jalen once every block-period (six to eight times per day). So, what does this 4:1 ratio look like with these three students as well as with all the other students in your classroom? Simply use your instincts about each student, your expertise about the principle of reinforcement, and your understanding of proportionality to achieve the 4:1 ratio. Based on current levels of behavioral performance, you know that you have a reasonably long period of time to catch most of your kids on their best behavior. Their low (or even nonexistent) levels of undesired behavior grant you larger blocks of time within which to achieve the 4:1 ratio. It wouldn't hurt to reinforce the others in your classroom for prosocial behavior on a more frequent basis, but the point is that you have the luxury of more time with most of your kids based on their current levels of performance. The time interval for Zoe is a bit more prescribed; her average daily rate of undesired behavior (her "baseline") suggests that you may have up to a full day in which to catch Zoe doing things the right way on at least four occasions. The time interval for Darius is tighter; you need to have him on your radar screen four times in the morning and four times in the afternoon in order to achieve the 4:1 ratio. Based on his established pattern, you will need to systematically attend to Jalen much more frequently; you must catch him doing things the correct way four times every block period in order to achieve the 4:1 ratio

Students	Period 1	Period 2	Period 3	Period 4	Period 5	Period 6
Zoe	😐 👍	👍	👍		👍	
Darius	😐 👍 👍	👍	👍	😐 👍	👍 👍	👍
Jalen	😐 👍 👍 👍 👍	😐 👍 👍 👍 👍	😐 👍 👍 👍 👍	😐 👍 👍 👍 👍	😐 👍 👍 👍	😐 👍 👍 👍

Figure 7.1.   The 4:1 ratio for three students across a six-period school day. (*Key:* 😐 = redirection; 👍 = positive reinforcement.)

and increase desired behavior over the longer term. Yes, for the record, Jalen appears to be a "kiddo with higher needs" in this regard. Figure 7.1 provides a visual representation of these varying intervals of reinforcement for Zoe, Darius, and Jalen throughout the school day.

This type of differentiation in your professional practice is based on student need, not personal preference. In other words, you are not favoring one student over another; you are professionally differentiating your instructional practice based on your understanding of your students' needs. What is consistent across all students in your class is achievement of the targeted 4:1 ratio. What varies is the time interval within which you are working, which is based on your students' needs.

Now, you may be wondering, "Will the other kids who are not getting behavior-specific reinforcement as frequently as Zoe, Darius, and Jalen rebel?" Well, it really depends on your ability to meet each of their needs for acknowledgment on an ongoing basis. If your proportionality of reinforcement does not address each of their needs for acknowledgment, those other kids may indeed rebel (in various ways). If they begin to feel like they are being taken for granted, you are likely to see more frequent nuisance (and perhaps problem) behavior. Should that situation arise, simply shorten the time interval for reinforcement of appropriate behavior for that particular student for a brief period of time.

> What is consistent across all students in your class is achievement of the targeted 4:1 ratio. What varies is the time interval within which you are working, which is based on each student's needs.

Desired behavior by your other kids who have been (at least to date) behaviorally successful is likely to continue as long as they feel they are being

acknowledged in a meaningful way. Sure, occasionally you may have one particular student who begins to voice their displeasure in a way that requires
you to pull them aside for a private talk. But as long
as each of your students (in a general sense) feels
as if they are being acknowledged at a level that is
reasonable from their perspective, significant problems are unlikely to surface. Here is the bottom
line: All your kids need reinforcement, but not all of
them need reinforcement at the same exact time or
on the same exact schedule. The goal is to achieve
the 4:1 ratio with each of your students as well as
with your class as a whole.

Here is the bottom line: All your kids need reinforcement, but not all of them need reinforcement at the same exact time or on the same exact schedule. The goal is to achieve the 4:1 ratio with each of your students as well as with your class as a whole.

The practice of providing group contingencies is another way to reinforce desired behavior, but instead of being applied individually, it is applied to a group of
students to support their behavior simultaneously. One benefit of group contingencies is that they can be implemented easily during naturally occurring activities (e.g.,
large-group instruction, independent work, centers, transition times) and can produce classwide outcomes efficiently. Group contingencies are most effective when
targeting behaviors that children already exhibit independently but are not using as
often as desired.

Suppose that you are teaching eighth-grade physical science. Your class as a whole
is struggling with meeting your expectations about being prepared at the beginning of
class. You decide to incorporate a group contingency system. In addition to delivering
behavior-specific praise (maybe something along the lines of "Wow! Nice job, Period 4,
for showing me you are prepared to get started today. I like that I am seeing so many of
you with your iPads open to the class notes already!"), you also place a class ticket into
a jar when 80% of the class shows they are prepared (e.g., science homework turned in,
iPad turned on with notes page ready for the day, science textbook on the desk). Establish a set of criteria with the class and a particular group reward to work toward, and
then increase the group contingency goal over time as the class consistently meets the
criteria. Building in classwide behavior-specific praise and/or reinforcement systems
is another avenue for achieving the 4:1 ratio classwide.

To illustrate, in one particular PBIS school, SOAR (Safe, Organized, Attentive,
and Responsible) cards are used. Students can earn SOAR cards for meeting schoolwide expectations. Suppose that Ms. Lopez sets a class goal of earning 10 SOAR cards;
students then choose by vote from a menu of reward options (e.g.,
pizza party, ice cream social, pajama day). In addition, individual
reinforcement opportunities exist, as students individually
earn SOAR cards for meeting expectations.

This 4:1 ratio, by the way, is not an arbitrary number
or concept. It is based on practical experiences and is a
logical extension of what has proved effective in the literature (OSEP, 2015). Specifically, the 4:1 ratio reflects a
similar proportionality as the 80%/20% split of prevention to intervention discussed in Chapter 4. To help you
put this concept into practice, Appendices E and F provide
descriptions of simple self-monitoring procedures relevant to

achieving the 4:1 ratio in your classroom. Consider using one of these methods (or a similar approach) to periodically self-monitor your reinforcement practices within your classroom. In addition to these paper-and-pencil techniques, some helpful apps can also assist you with your reinforcement schedule, such as Be + (Be Positive) (https://www.pbis.org/announcements/track-positive-reinforcement-with-our-be-app), Behavior Tracker Pro (https://www.behaviortrackerpro.com/), and On Task (https://www.ontaskapp.com/).

HOW DO I DETERMINE WHICH REINFORCERS ARE APPROPRIATE?

Now that you have a working sense of the importance of acknowledging desired behavior through positive reinforcement, it is important to select reinforcers that are appropriate to use with your students. As mentioned previously, what any one particular student finds reinforcing is relative. Some prefer public praise, and others want to keep it private. To identify things that your students find desirable (besides your attention), you may be able to pull from information already collected if you happen to be teaching in a PBIS school. If you teach in a more traditional setting, you may need to gather this type of information on your own. There are many different ways to identify potential reinforcers. The most important thing to understand is that there is no preordained set of universal reinforcers—no one-size-fits-all solutions. Remember, what works with one student may not work with another. It can be helpful to vary the reinforcers that you use to capitalize on what is referred to as the "novelty effect"—as the old saying goes, "Variety is the spice of life." Keep in mind that any given reinforcer can lose power over time. Be prepared to change things up to keep your students' interest and motivation high, and always have your next-in-line reinforcers ready to roll. Table 7.2 provides four commonly used approaches to identifying reinforcers for use in your classroom.

Now that you are feeling more confident in REAPing the benefits of a trauma-informed approach to classroom management (in building strong **R**apport with your students, **E**stablishing clear expectations reflecting SEL, and **A**cknowledging appropriate behaviors through varied and individualized reinforcement methods), let's move on to the fourth and final cornerstone of preventive practice: **P**roviding increased opportunities for student engagement. Increasing engagement will encourage your students to participate and be on-task more often, making your classroom climate exude increasing degrees of positivity and liveliness.

Table 7.2. Common approaches to identifying reinforcers

Strategy	Description
Watch and learn	Observe your students during situations in which they have freedom of choice in activities and with whom they interact. To paraphrase Yogi Berra, "You can see a lot by looking." Gain a sense of the things (stimuli) that your kids find enjoyable based on the choices that they make during situations such as free time, recess, and other nonacademic settings and routines.
Reinforcer inventory: borrow and adapt, or create your own	**Borrow and adapt** You may be working in a program with an adopted curriculum that already includes reinforcement inventories for your use. Or, you may engage in the well-known "beg, borrow, and steal" approach so you don't have to reinvent the wheel; use what has worked well for others by asking colleagues for advice and resources or looking for them on your own. There may be some already developed inventories you can use or modify to suit your needs. A simple Google search or looking into reinforcement survey apps can lead you to a host of options. **Create your own** Create a list of potential reinforcers in the format of a checklist and/or questionnaire. Use a Likert-type scale (e.g., 1 to 5, with 1 being *least desired* and 5 being *most desired*) when developing the inventory. Then, have your students independently complete the inventory and review the results to gain insight into what they report. Remember that what is reported on an inventory is not always consistent with what that student may actually do in real-life situations. Some of your students may simply respond by reporting things that they think you want them to say.
Interview students	Sit down and talk with your students (or their parents/caregivers) in groups and/or one on one. Ask them about the types of things that make them feel good and/or proud, as well as things that would represent their worst nightmare (in terms of the classroom). Like inventories, verbal or written self-reports are not as reliable or accurate as actually seeing what a student does (remember the old maxim, "Do as I say and not as I do").
Use your best guess or trial and error	Think about the ages and cultural backgrounds of your students. Specifically, what types of things are other students of similar age and backgrounds interested in? What are their activities of choice? Try some of these in the classroom (combine with "watch and learn") and use the process of elimination to identify the most powerful reinforcers to add to your menu of options. Keep a record of the success of the various reinforcers you have tried so you can refer back to these when attempting new reinforcers.

REFLECTIVE EXERCISE

During this school year, you have been focusing heavily on providing sufficient levels of behavior-specific praise with your class as a whole and on achieving a 4:1 ratio with each student on a consistent basis. However, you struggle to achieve these goals with Cameron. During every class period, you find yourself redirecting Cameron for problem-level behavior—nothing too dangerous but sufficiently problematic that it requires direct intervention. Examples include Cameron being off task far too long and disrupting others from completing their work.

Based on this scenario, and reflecting on what you have read in this chapter, complete the final column in Figure 7.2 concerning Cameron.

Current frequency (baseline) of problem behavior requiring redirection with Cameron	Times during each class period I will target Cameron to catch meeting expectations to provide behavior-specific praise
On average, one time each class period	1.
	2.
	3.
	4.

Figure 7.2.   Reflective exercise on Cameron.

8

Providing Increased Opportunities for Student Engagement

Providing increased opportunities for student engagement is essential to establishing a positive learning environment in your classroom and serves as the fourth cornerstone in our REAP foundation. Student engagement can be increased by providing structured *opportunities to respond (OTRs)*. OTRs are essential in constructing opportunities to deliver positive reinforcement when students meet expectations. Both personal experience and the literature clearly indicate that students tend to demonstrate improved academic achievement and fewer behavioral problems when teachers integrate OTRs within the ebb and flow of classroom instruction (Simonsen et al., 2008). Providing varied and frequent OTRs can prove particularly helpful for students who have experienced trauma. Helping students feel included and their voices literally "heard" becomes even more empowering over time. By providing a range of OTRs, you are fostering classroom engagement in a way that is sensitive to trauma and promotes many of the core SAMHSA principles that have been touched on throughout this book (see Figure 4.2).

> Providing varied and frequent OTRs can prove particularly helpful for students who have experienced trauma.

When you reflect back on your own favorite teachers, it is likely that their classrooms were active in some way, providing multiple opportunities for student engagement. One of our favorite teachers was Mrs. T. Mrs. T exuded positivity in every interaction with her students, as well as a distinct passion for her content area (math). She was extremely attentive to student needs, and the level of empathy and acceptance she showed rarely went unnoticed. Mrs. T taught high school students math across all academic levels, from remedial math through advanced algebra. Her instruction regularly engaged students in practicing skills in a variety of ways, and she always integrated real-world applications to make the concepts interesting and relevant. Mrs. T knew just how to challenge each student; when the going got tough, she was always right there to encourage and provide support until it "clicked." Mrs. T made it her priority to invest in all of her students and see them succeed, even those who were not confident in math or who were at the point of shutting out most teachers based on past school experiences. She communicated clear expectations for participation and provided a range of opportunities for students to engage in her lessons that aligned

> The more your students are directly engaged through responding to questions and completing tasks, the more readily opportunities will surface for providing positive reinforcement.

with the participation preferences of her students, whether that was oral responses during class, working with partners on practice activities, working independently and receiving individual feedback, or coming up to the board to share their work. Such high levels of engagement kept her students interested and made each one of them feel like a valued part of the learning community.

The literature is clear on the power of student engagement. Back in the early 1990s (which may sound like an eternity ago to some of you Gen Zs, Alphas, and beyond), Skinner and Belmont (1993) observed the relationship between teacher practices and active student engagement. They discovered a cycle in which higher levels of student engagement related to more frequent positive teacher behavior, which resulted in more actively engaged students. On the flipside, the reverse cycle occurred when low levels of engagement were observed. The less students were engaged, the more negative teacher behaviors were observed, which in turn suppressed student well-being, learning, and engagement. The translation of these findings is as follows: The more your students are directly engaged through responding to questions and completing tasks, the more readily opportunities will surface for providing positive reinforcement. In addition, the more you engage your students through OTRs, the less students will engage in undesired behavior.

Although providing high rates of OTRs is relevant for all of your students, it is particularly helpful for students who are struggling. Research indicates that when students struggling behaviorally or academically are provided with increasing OTRs, myriad benefits emerge; these include improved reading and math skills, greater time on task, and decreases in disruptive behavior (Sutherland & Wehby, 2001). New methods of engagement can open up more opportunities for students to feel heard and be more active in their learning. Approaching student engagement through this trauma-informed lens can be groundbreaking with your most hard-to-reach kiddos.

HOW OFTEN IS OFTEN ENOUGH IN PROVIDING OPPORTUNITIES TO RESPOND?

The research varies in terms of how many OTRs to provide within a targeted time frame. With new content, four to six OTRs per minute with a goal of 80% accuracy in student responses has been suggested. When reviewing already-learned materials, the response rate can be increased to 8 to 12 per minute with a higher accuracy of 90% (CEC, 1987). Other sources have suggested providing at least three OTRs per minute with new content for the greatest impact on student academic and behavioral growth (Scott et al., 2011). Obviously, these rates apply to responses that are quicker to elicit such as verbal answers or simple action responses. For more complex responses, less-frequent rates are more realistic. The key takeaway is to provide reasonably frequent, quality OTRs. Appendix I includes a resource for self-monitoring your OTRs.

> The key takeaway is to provide reasonably frequent, quality OTRs.

WHAT STRATEGIES CAN I ADD TO MY OPPORTUNITIES TO RESPOND TOOLBOX?

A range of strategies is available to support your efforts to provide a sufficient level of OTRs to reach all learners. According to Archer and Hughes (2011), response opportunities fall into three broad categories: say (oral), write (written), and do (action).

Say (Oral)

The say (oral) category is composed of both individual and unison responses. In an effort to hear from a large number of students and incorporate a variety of question types, you can use both individual and unison responses depending on your targeted student learning outcomes. Individual oral responses can be elicited when you want to touch on higher levels of challenge or critical thinking (think of the Apply or Analyze levels of Bloom's Taxonomy, or Level 4 of Webb's Depth of Knowledge). Individual responses also engage students in making personal connections and reflections. Unison or choral responses are useful in engaging a wider range of students and maximizing overall response opportunities. If you want to elicit a brief unison response, pose questions for which most of the class would likely respond with the same word or phrase. Having students respond in unison may take a little modeling and practice, but it can be a refreshing new way for students to participate instead of calling on the same handful of steadfast volunteers every time you ask a question. Regardless of the type of "say" response you elicit, the procedures outlined in Table 8.1 will help you be more efficient and attentive to student needs as you promote student engagement.

Many of the strategies for "say" (oral) responses work well within the context of a face-to-face setting. When teaching virtually, think through your expectations for student participation and explicitly teach and reinforce them. Walk students through various actions or tools they should use to participate and provide them with immediate feedback on their use of those actions/tools. During live virtual instruction, the muting and unmuting of microphones, along with confusion related to hand raising and chat responses, can add up to a chaotic and disorganized learning environment. Be clear with your students in advance about how you want them to participate during virtual lessons (e.g., instructing them to use the raise hand icon to volunteer a response or explicitly telling them when it is permissible to add responses into the chat box). Be consistent in reinforcing those expectations.

Here is an illustration. Mr. Jackson was testing out some ways to engage more students on Microsoft Teams during live lessons, so he decided to implement a whole-class response method. This response method, which he called a "Waterfall Chat and Share," involved all students responding on cue and in unison to a prompt given by the teacher; Mr. Jackson then selected a few students to share out and expand on their responses. Because he had not yet tested out this new response method in his class, Mr. Jackson invested time in explicitly describing what it was, identifying the steps with which students would participate, and emphasizing the cue they would wait for until they hit "send" to submit their unison responses. This level of clarity in expectations, paired with a quick check for understanding before beginning the activity, resulted in high levels of engagement; some students who typically did not participate in class were able to share their thoughts alongside those of their peers.

Table 8.1. Steps for eliciting student responses

Steps	Additional tips
1. Ask your question.	Provide a little precorrection if working with young students or students who frequently call out; ask them to raise a quiet hand (or follow whatever expectation you have set for participating).
2. Provide sufficient wait time.	The generally accepted wait time is 3–5 seconds (the "awkward" pause, so to speak) to provide sufficient think time for students to process your question and formulate their response. This wait time is a great way to provide additional support, not only for students who need more cognitive processing time but also for those who are often hesitant to raise their hands; a few extra seconds could provide them with more confidence to put together and share their thoughts.

3. Cue your response.
 	
   a. If eliciting an individual response, call on a student by name.
   b. If eliciting a unison response, use a verbal cue or gesture to signal a succinct response.
	Calling on a volunteer to share is fine as long as you make mental notes about the variety of students you are calling on and use the wait time to encourage more willing volunteers.
	
	Shake things up by calling on a non-volunteer. One point that is particularly relevant to trauma-informed approaches is to apply caution when randomly calling on a student who requires longer than the typical wait time for processing or one who was off task. Strategies include use of Popsicle sticks, the "whip and pass" method for rapid factor responses from every student, or a website that randomly selects students using a wheel of names spinner or picking a name out of a virtual hat (a quick Google search can reveal online spinners and pickers and other creative options).
	
	Use the verbal cue "Everyone," possibly paired with a gesture to assist in the delivery of a crisp and cohesive choral response from your group. Some teachers use a gesture such as a lowering of a hand, pointing to the class, or a snap-to signal that a unison response is desired. Model and practice with students initially so they are able to meet your expectations for unison delivery. If you are not getting a cohesive response, or if not all are responding, firm up your response by repeating the question and signal to remind students of the expectation for all to participate.

4. Provide immediate feedback to students.	Reinforce correct responses with behavior-specific praise or guide students by providing explicit error correction if responses are not on target.

Write (Written)

Write (written responses) is another common method used to engage students. Whether your students use traditional paper-and-pencil methods (e.g., entrance or exit slips—which also could be done virtually through Google or Office Forms) or dry-erase boards, whiteboards on iPads, or mini chalk boards during guided practice exercises, be sure to provide clear directions and immediate feedback. When teaching virtually, use of a shared screen or collaborative virtual whiteboard (e.g., through a platform like Zoom or another online app such as FigJam by Figma or Lucidspark by Lucid) can be another tool for generating written responses in real time.

If you have students come up to the board to write out a response (e.g., a math equation), to enhance student success be sure to provide think-time as was mentioned previously for say responses, possibly paired with some time to jot down notes or work out their answer first. Perhaps one of your students requires more time to process information; imagine their elevated anxiety level when they are called up to the board

to solve a long-division problem on the spot. Always remember that greater levels of participation through your OTRs are intended to promote student success. Coming up to the board can be a highly engaging and motivating opportunity for many students, especially younger learners who may eagerly enjoy this time in the spotlight, but that is not true for all students. Always be cognizant of the reinforcer preferences mentioned in Chapter 7: What is reinforcing to one student may not be reinforcing to another. For students who experience high levels of anxiety, that extra wait/think-time and possibly some advanced notice prior to being called up to the board may be crucial in setting them up for success. You may need to have alternative approaches to coming up to the board to participate in front of the class. Think about your ultimate goal with respect to having any particular student come up to participate at the board. There are usually alternative ways for students to show you what they know. Your flexibility in meeting students where they are will not go unnoticed and should strengthen the trust and rapport you are building with your students.

> Always remember that greater levels of participation through your OTRs is intended to promote student success.

Do (Action)

The final category of OTRs is the "do" or action response. The increasing integration of technology in both face-to-face and virtual classroom settings has broadened the range of fun and creative methods for you to consider in attempting to increase student engagement. Student response systems (e.g., clickers) or evolving technologies easily accessible through cell phones or tablets allow students of all ages and ability levels to engage individually or collaboratively as a member of a team. We are sure that many of you recognize the increase in energy levels in a classroom when a Kahoot! is opened up, particularly for younger students or novice users of such applications. This and other interactive methods for participation and lesson presentation provide a multitude of options to shuffle in and out of your toolkit. In addition to Kahoot!, there are similar programs like Quizziz, Formative (also known as GoFormative), Nearpod, Blooket, or Socrative—the list goes on and on. The key is to be selective in choosing how to integrate technology in your classroom.

There are a number of helpful resources to assist in technology integration. One is the Technological Pedagogical Content Knowledge (TPACK) framework (Mishra & Koehler, 2006). TPACK assists educators in ensuring they focus on core content essential for their students to learn, teach it using high-quality pedagogical practices, and weave in technological tools that match and promote instruction and student learning. The key is to make purposeful choices about which forms of technology will best enhance your provision of OTRs. Try to avoid overloading students with too many new and flashy programs, which can be quite overwhelming and counterproductive. Sometimes, good old response cards, Popsicle sticks, or hand gestures (e.g., holding up a *1, 2,* or *3* for an answer) work just as well as, or even better than, a new tech tool (see Appendices G and H for two basic reproducible student response card sheets). If you prefer a balance between low tech and high tech, consider Plickers, which combines the use of a response card along with a mobile app that can be accessed for data collection purposes.

In addition, consider ways to get your students up and moving around the room in this interactive response category of OTRs. Action thermometers allow students to stand along a continuum to represent their response preference or comfort level after a scenario is given. Or, vocabulary can be acted out in a game similar to charades. Regardless of the type of interactive response you choose, make sure to engage in precorrection: walk your students through what they are expected to do before beginning an activity. Imagine the chaos that could ensue, and the endless cacophony of "What do we do? I don't understand! Where is the button we click on?" and so forth, that could emerge when your students engage in a new activity without instructions. We cannot overstate the importance of providing explicit expectations and clear directions in advance for your students to engage in active learning.

> Finding new ways to reach and empower your students to be active participants in the learning process can be a game changer with your less-engaged students.

By now, we hope that you are feeling more empowered and better equipped to provide increased student engagement through OTRs. Spend some time looking through your curriculum and use what you know about your students' interests to select methods that will really connect with them and excite them about engaging in their learning. Finding new ways to reach and empower your students to be active participants in the learning process can be a game changer with your less-engaged students. Pairing increased engagement with positive reinforcement can further enhance student success.

So, now you know about **REAP:** 1) **R**apport building, 2) **E**stablishing behavioral expectations reflecting SEL, 3) **A**cknowledging desired behaviors, and 4) **P**roviding increased opportunities for student engagement. As with cornerstones, each of these principles of practice is important in its own right, but the foundation is strongest when they are all implemented in alignment. No one wall of a new home can support the entire dwelling. Similarly, these components of preventive classroom management are each rendered more effective when aligned with one another. This trauma-informed approach to prevention can help you establish a dynamic environment conducive to learning and subsequently a welcoming classroom climate for everyone. Remember, the whole is worth more than the sum of its parts.

> Remember, the whole is worth more than the sum of its parts.

REFLECTIVE EXERCISE

You have been becoming increasingly frustrated. Your students appear disinterested in the curriculum and less engaged than you desire throughout instruction. Even though you are not experiencing any major disciplinary problems, at least not right now, you need to find a way to energize and engage your students in the classroom.

Based on this scenario, and reflecting on what you learned in this chapter, complete the middle and right-hand columns of Figure 8.1.

Possible OTR menu of options to implement	OTR strategies I will target with brief descriptions	Goal for frequency of OTRs
Say (individual and unison responses)		
Write (paper-and-pencil, whiteboard, dry-erase board, or virtual options)		
Do (student response systems, e.g., clickers, iPads/laptop/cell phone applications such as Kahoot!, or response cards)		

Figure 8.1.   Reflective exercise on student engagement. (*Key:* OTR, opportunity to respond.)

9

Addressing Undesired Behavior

As more and more educators learn about trauma and ACEs, many teachers begin to call into question some of their past instructional practices. This, by itself, is not a bad thing. Professional reflection is very helpful for continued professional growth. However, when teachers call into question those practices to the point that they hesitate to establish structure out of fear of retraumatizing their students, it can have a negative impact on the classroom environment. Let us begin by unequivocally stating that providing proactive, preventive structures such as those highlighted throughout this book—including redirecting undesired behavior—does not in and of itself equate to retraumatizing students. To the contrary, one of the core features of a trauma-informed classroom is for students to feel physically and emotionally safe within the learning environment. The issue is not *whether* educators should provide such preventive structure (e.g., establishing expectations reflecting SEL) and intervene in response to undesired student behavior. Instead, the issue is *how* these interventions should be delivered. Consideration of the impact of those procedures on the students and on the broader learning environment is essential.

HOW DO I REDIRECT UNDESIRED BEHAVIOR IN A TRAUMA-INFORMED WAY?

This is a very understandable, and important, question. The trauma-informed preventive approaches that you have learned about so far should prove to be effective with most of your students. However, even in the best of circumstances, there will likely be some students who will require periodic redirection.

It is important to have both a short-term view and a long-term view when redirecting a student's behavior. The short-term view is, of course, constructive, trauma-informed redirection of a particular student's behavior at a given moment in time. However, it is equally important to keep the long-term view in mind, which is related to the issue of equity. The way in which you redirect student behavior has implications with respect to equity, particularly when you think about disciplinary consequences that may emerge.

When considering matters of equity, it is important to apply a functional lens to your assessment of a student's behavior. Remember that behavior is not random in nature. Instead, it serves a purpose, or function, for the student. In other words, don't limit your perspective on a given student's undesired behavior to what it looks like or sounds like. There are varying degrees of functional behavioral assessment (FBA) in schools, ranging from applying that functional lens throughout the day in your classroom to a formal FBA conducted by a student-centered educational team that leads to the development of a multicomponent behavior support plan. In this chapter, we focus on how you view the behavior of your students throughout a typical day.

Before we explore the details of redirection procedures, know that it is important to be conscious of emerging patterns of behavior with your students, keeping equity clearly in mind. Apply a functional trauma-informed lens to your assessment of student behavior. In reality, it is unlikely that you will be able to realize the development of prosocial skills with a particular student who is struggling if you rely heavily on reactive, consequence-oriented practices. Yes, during a crisis-level situation, an immediate, reactive strategy may be necessary to protect the health and well-being of students and staff. However, such crisis-level situations are rare, as should be reliance on such approaches. Be proactive, keep an eye open for patterns that may begin to emerge with particular students, and increase your frequency of use of preventive approaches (REAP).

WHAT IS THE DIFFERENCE BETWEEN NUISANCE-LEVEL BEHAVIOR AND PROBLEM-LEVEL BEHAVIOR?

Before we get into the specifics of redirecting student behavior, it is important to differentiate between *nuisance-level behavior* and *problem-level behavior,* because each warrants a different type of response. As the old saying goes, do not make a mountain out of a molehill (i.e., overreact to nuisance-level behavior). That said, you do not want minor waves in your classroom pool (nuisance-level behavior) to become behavioral tsunamis (problem-level behavior). Remember, how you respond to both nuisance-level and problem-level behaviors will take place in the

context of your overall trauma-informed approach to classroom operations. As teachers, we instruct through our actions as well as our curriculum, which includes modeling how to respond to actions by others that create stressful situations. Your students are always watching!

As a reminder, nuisance-level behaviors are the things kids do that (although somewhat bothersome) are inconsequential. In other words, if you pulled the actual undesired behavior out of context and looked at it in isolation (in a vacuum or under a proverbial microscope), the actual behavior would likely not look like a big deal. However, in the classroom, nuisance-level behaviors can really wear you down over time. For example, frequent minor occurrences of off-task behavior by Amir or a group of his peers can really get on your nerves—thus the importance of self-management of instructional practice.

Nuisance-level behavior is best addressed through indirect intervention. Do not call attention to a student engaged in nuisance behavior. There are generally two types of situations in which you may need to systematically ignore nuisance behavior:

- **One-to-one situation.** You could simply not respond to Amir's nuisance behavior… as if you did not see it. This is often referred to as *planned ignoring*. Rather, focus on things he is doing correctly and avoid providing visible attention toward those other behaviors (e.g., fidgeting, perseverations, or brief moments of off-task behavior).

- **Group instructional situation.** When Amir engages in nuisance-level behavior in a group, simply find other students who are engaged in desired behaviors who are in close physical proximity. Keep Amir on your radar screen in a way that does not suggest you are watching him. In other words, keep an eye on him without him realizing it. Reinforce those other students one at a time for appropriate behavior while not responding to Amir's nuisance behavior. Next, capitalize on the opportunity to "catch him being good" by explicitly reinforcing Amir for appropriate behavior once he ceases the nuisance behavior and engages in desired behavior (e.g., on-task behavior).

In both of these illustrations, the key strategy is to appear to ignore the student's nuisance-level behavior rather than feeding into it while using the reinforcement procedures first described in Chapter 7 to promote desired behavior. Using this approach (responding indirectly) should help position you to act in a manner consistent with the preventive approaches previously highlighted and achieve the 80%/20% balance.

It is important to apply a compassionate eye when identifying nuisance-level behavior. This is particularly the case if the behavior is simply not within the student's ability to fully self-regulate. Examples include responses associated with an underlying physical or emotional condition, such as motor tics associated with Tourette syndrome. In such instances, it is important to respect this type of diversity to help you and all of your students navigate such situations in a time-efficient way that contributes to a positive learning environment. Careful handling of these situations can serve as invaluable life lessons for your students and can expand on the already-established expectations reflecting SEL. In addition, such demonstrations of compassion will likely enhance your rapport-building efforts with the student of concern.

> Nuisance (inconsequential) behavior is best addressed through indirect intervention.

Behavior ceases to be inconsequential when it becomes disruptive or potentially harmful. Examples include 1) a student being off task for a time that is longer than reasonable despite your efforts to intervene indirectly as described previously, 2) behavior that pulls other kids off task or creates a physically or emotionally unsafe situation and 3) the behavior places that student or others in harm's way. When such problem-level behavior or consequential behavior occurs, you should intervene directly by employing a basic three-step redirection process:

1. Tell the student to stop the problem behavior (e.g., name-calling, being out of their seat, interrupting classmates).

2. Direct the student to perform a more desired behavior.

3. Reinforce the student once they comply with your redirection.

Table 9.1. Three-part script to redirect a student's problem-level behavior

Step in process	What to say
Part 1 When Cheyenne engages in problem behavior, directly intervene by getting in reasonable physical proximity—not too close but not too far away—and assertively stopping her from continuing the problem-level behavior.	Tell the student to stop the behavior. Be specific and label it (e.g., "Cheyenne, stop grabbing Kai's materials off his desk").
Part 2 Once you have gained Cheyenne's attention with your "stop" statement, redirect her to an alternative behavior that is in keeping with your established expectations.	State the alternative behavior (e.g., "Take a deep breath, let go of Kai's book, and keep your hands on your own materials and start doing your work").
Part 3 Once you have redirected Cheyenne, pause and wait for her to respond. If she does not comply, simply repeat your verbal redirection, adding additional prompts and cues if needed to enable compliance. Once compliance occurs, provide reinforcement for following your redirection.	Provide explicit verbal praise for compliance (e.g., "Thank you, Cheyenne, for using your own materials and doing your work").

Regarding this third step: you are not reinforcing the student for the problem behavior, but you are reinforcing them for compliance with your redirection when they perform the alternative appropriate behavior. Be sure to be explicit about what you are reinforcing by providing behavior-specific praise. When using a direct intervention, keep your words and actions to a minimum; this allows you to be efficient with your time while observing how the student responds.

> When using a direct intervention, keep your words and actions to a minimum; this allows you to be efficient with your time while observing how the student responds.

Provide corrective feedback (when needed) in as private a manner as possible to minimize the likelihood of public power struggles or embarrassment. Table 9.1 outlines a basic three-part script to consider when redirecting student behavior.

WHAT SHOULD I LOOK FOR BASED ON MY REDIRECTION?

As mentioned previously in the chapter, certain behavior patterns with particular students may emerge over time. Although many students respond positively to the combination of preventive and interventive procedures described so far, others may not respond as desired. This may be the case immediately with students experiencing mental health challenges. We address the needs of this particular population of students in Chapter 10. However, for the purpose of general redirection procedures, the important takeaway at this juncture is to be observant for patterns that may emerge with particular students. Depending on your level of concern, it may also prove helpful to record the frequency, intensity, and duration of a student's behaviors of concern.

> Be observant for patterns that may emerge with particular students.

The key to using redirection procedures efficiently is in making them become proportionally habitual within the ebb and flow of the daily activities in your classroom. We all develop habits; the key is in developing effective ones. The goal is to move beyond the initial acquisition phase (in which thinking and walking through a procedure is a cognitive task) to the point at which their use becomes associative and you operate on muscle memory to some degree. There is no shortcut we are aware of in moving from acquisition to fluency. The key is preparation through practice (ideally through simulated activities with your colleagues), followed by consistent application and professional reflection. You might even lean into the effective practice of video self-reflection to witness and reflect on your personal growth.

Although practice doesn't always make perfect when it comes to real-life situations, it can help you be more prepared. So, do yourself a favor and *practice, practice, practice* in advance. One of our mentors, Dr. Wolfe, always stressed in her courses, "Practice makes permanent." Over time, use of these procedures can become time-efficient when you need to redirect undesired student behavior. Making routine use of these procedures can be particularly helpful when a student engages in a form of undesired behavior that is particularly and personally aggravating to you (one of your own personal triggers, so to speak), or on a day when you are not feeling particularly resilient.

Practice makes permanent.

WHAT IS A VULNERABLE DECISION-MAKING POINT, AND HOW SHOULD I HANDLE IT?

Regarding those times when you feel less resilient, maybe because of a cold or feeling run-down, we all experience what have been referred to as *vulnerable decision-making points,* or VDPs (McIntosh et al., 2014). A VDP is a specific decision that must be made at a point in time when you are more vulnerable to the effects of implicit bias. VDPs are composed of two parts: 1) your own personal decision-making state, or internal state, such as feeling tired or your feelings based on prior experiences, and 2) the situation within which the decision must be made. For educators, redirecting a student engaged in undesired behavior is one of the situations susceptible to implicit bias. This bias can in turn feed into disproportionality in official school disciplinary actions (e.g., suspensions).

It is important to be observant of your own patterns of behavior as well as those of your students. If you notice a pattern emerging (e.g., you are redirecting particular students more frequently, resulting in more office discipline referrals), you may be at a VDP and need to establish what is referred to as a "neutralizing routine." As highlighted

It is important to be observant of your own patterns of behavior as well as those of your students.

by McIntosh and colleagues (2014), essential features of a good neutralizing routine are brevity and utilization of *if–then* type statements to guide actions (e.g., *if* this is a VDP, *then* I may need to think for a moment about alternative responses before sending the student to the office). Another feature of a good neutralizing routine is that it is doable, meaning that it is practical for ongoing use as needed in the classroom. One result of a neutralizing routine might be delaying the final decision on the disciplinary consequence following redirection for undesired behavior, using the least exclusionary consequence available. This positions you to have a more private discussion with the student within a reasonable time following the occurrence of the undesired behavior. When experiencing a VDP in a team-teaching setting, it may prove helpful to hand off the determination of consequences to a colleague who was not directly involved in the situation.

The need to periodically redirect undesired student behavior is inevitable in any classroom, regardless of whether your trauma-informed classroom is part of a school employing an MTSS framework or a more traditional school setting. Fluency in both indirect and direct intervention is essential to your success in the classroom. Always remember that your primary objective at the moment of indirect or direct intervention is to simply redirect the student of concern (e.g., Amir or Cheyenne) to engage in appropriate (desired) behavior and to provide behavior-specific praise for desired behavior. To illustrate, think about a fire department (with trucks and firefighters) that arrives at a burning building. What if their initial actions were to stand around and talk about how the fire started and how to prevent fires from happening in the future? This, of course, makes no sense. The primary task at hand is to put out the fire to minimize immediate damage. Discussing the origin of the fire and how to prevent reoccurrence in the future should prove very helpful, but that conversation should occur later on. This is precisely how redirection procedures operate. When redirecting a student, your primary objective is to get the "fire" to stop by constructively directing them to a more desired course of action at that moment in time. Keeping this clearly in mind will help you self-manage your instructional practice more effectively when you need to redirect a student for undesired behavior.

> When redirecting a student, your primary objective is to get the "fire" to stop by directing them to a more desired course of action at that moment in time.

IS REDIRECTION ALONE A LONG-TERM SOLUTION?

Remember: Even with all you now know about redirection procedures, you may still encounter a student who requires redirection on an increasing basis. This does not necessarily mean you are making mistakes; on the contrary, the student's compliance with redirection at a given moment in time indicates that the procedure you used had the immediate desired effect. However, effective use of redirection procedures will accomplish only short-term effects. Redirection procedures should not be viewed as sufficient in and of themselves to increase instances of future desired behavior. By design, their intent is to simply "put out the fire at that moment in time."

When patterns of concerning behavior begin to emerge, that particular student's needs may require more investment in the trauma-informed preventive procedures highlighted in previous chapters (e.g., increased rapport building, reestablishment of the behavioral expectations reflecting SEL, providing a higher frequency of acknowledgment of desired behaviors to achieve the 4:1 ratio, and increasing engagement).

Should patterns of concern persist despite your good faith efforts to ramp-up your preventive approaches, consider integrating Tier 2 (targeted) strategies by building them on top of your universal preventive approaches. To be clear, addressing the needs of a student who is not sufficiently responding to your trauma-informed preventive approaches does not entail giving up on them. Instead, much like adding on additional layers of clothing when you are cold, you will need to strategically layer the Tier 2 approaches described in Chapter 11 on top of those universal trauma-informed practices to address that student's needs. But first, you need to know how a trauma-informed approach will benefit them as well as all students in your classroom as we will address in the next chapter.

REFLECTIVE EXERCISE

Your school has increasingly focused on issues related to disciplinary disproportionality. As a result, you have become aware of the importance of understanding VDPs and having neutralizing routines in place.

Based on this scenario, and reflecting on what you learned in this chapter about VDPs and neutralizing routines, review the example we have provided (see Figure 9.1) and create two additional illustrations using examples from your own experiences.

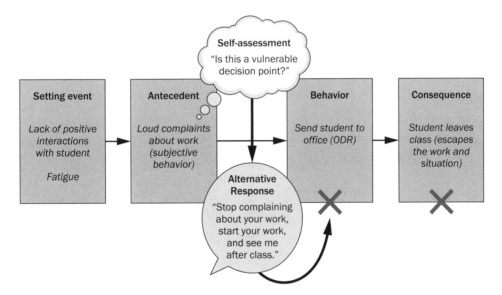

Figure 9.1. Sample completed reflective exercise on neutralizing routines. (*Key:* ODR, office discipline referrals.) (Adapted with permission from ReACT. © 2022 University of Oregon.)

Your Own Illustration (1)

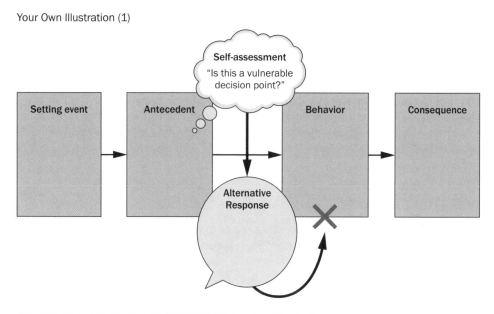

(Adapted with permission from ReACT. © 2022 University of Oregon.)

Your Own Illustration (2)

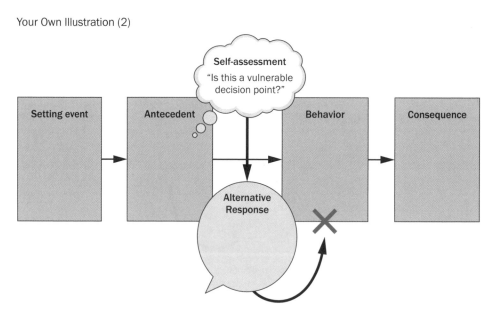

(Adapted with permission from ReACT. © 2022 University of Oregon.)

10

Helping Students With Mental Health and Wellness

Our primary emphasis throughout this book has been on universal (Tier 1) trauma-informed approaches in the classroom to support all students. The instructional practices highlighted in the previous chapters can be broadly applied to any instructional setting across all age and grade levels. They should help facilitate the social and emotional well-being of your students while creating a learning environment conducive to addressing the educational needs of students experiencing mental health challenges. We are not suggesting that universal approaches alone will be sufficient to meet the unique needs of students experiencing mental health challenges, such as a diagnosed mental illness. Instead, we suggest that operating a trauma-informed classroom will best position you to address more challenging situations with students who have more complex needs.

DO THE BASIC HUMAN NEEDS OF STUDENTS EXPERIENCING MENTAL HEALTH CHALLENGES DIFFER FROM THEIR PEERS?

The basic human needs of a student experiencing mental health challenges do not change fundamentally in the face of those challenges, even if they result in a diagnosed mental illness. Instead, the student's mental health challenges become part of who they are, contributing to their personal history or narrative. They do not change their essential human nature.

To expand on this notion, let's revisit a topic that is likely familiar to you: Maslow's hierarchy of needs (see Figure 10.1). Abraham Maslow established this way of organizing our thinking about human needs more than 60 years ago, but it still serves today as a bedrock of understanding.

Maslow's hierarchy is divided into what are referred to as *deficiency needs* and *growth needs*. The lower four levels of the hierarchy (physiological, safety, social, and esteem needs) are typically viewed as deficiency needs, with the top level (self-actualization) considered as growth needs.

> The basic human needs of a student experiencing mental health challenges do not change fundamentally in the face of those challenges, even if they result in a diagnosed mental illness.

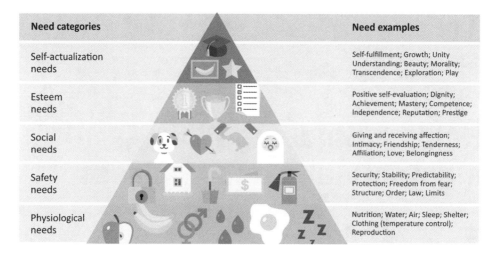

Figure 10.1.   Desmet and Fokkinga's (2020) pyramid representation of Maslow's hierarchy of needs. (From Desmet, P., & Fokkinga, S. [2020]. Beyond Maslow's pyramid: Introducing a typology of thirteen fundamental needs for human-centered design. *Multimodal Technologies and Interaction, 4*[3], 38; reprinted by permission.)

Deficiency suggests *deprivation*. Deficiency needs, which arise due to varying degrees of deprivation, understandably become a focal point of concern for the affected person. In essence, experiencing prolonged, significant deficiency needs can become a risk factor with respect to mental health challenges. For example, the longer a student is denied sufficient levels of nutritious food to meet their physiological needs, the hungrier they become over time. The student becomes (understandably) increasingly preoccupied with satisfying this need. Similarly, the longer a student feels disconnected, isolated, or marginalized (experiencing a deficiency related to their social needs), the greater the chance that they will feel increasingly sad or anxious.

Our schools have, to varying degrees, historically operated protective programs to address an array of basic needs of our students. Programs like breakfast, lunch, and after-school meal programs are often extended by community partnerships to include weekends, school breaks, and the summer months. Schools also provide various types of physical health–related services, including annual physical exams; hearing, vision, and dental screenings; and other preventive programs. Further, as educators, we all must adhere to mandated reporting requirements to help meet the safety needs of our students. Although perhaps not by conscious design, these types of programs are loosely trauma-informed and certainly help to address basic student needs.

As important as these broad-based programs are, they cannot sufficiently address the breadth and depth of needs of all students across all levels of Maslow's hierarchy on their own. There are many reasons for this shortcoming, none the fault per se of any particular specific program. Suffice it to say that inequities exist, particularly when it comes to addressing mental health challenges. If left unaddressed, these inequities may only become greater, a problem that is compounded by the growing numbers of students experiencing mental health challenges today. Systematically embedding trauma-informed approaches within the daily ebb and flow of both classroom and nonclassroom settings, along with such already established programs as mentioned previously, can lower the risk of trauma and other ACEs from emerging in the first place. Embedding trauma-informed approaches can also help mitigate the associated effects of mental health challenges.

Even as we acknowledge the relevance of Maslow's hierarchy, with particular focus on deficiency needs, it is important to appreciate that satisfying those needs is not an "all-or-nothing" proposition. A student can have needs across the entire hierarchy at any given point in time. Further, addressing needs at a higher level is not entirely dependent on completely satisfying those at a lower level. For example, an adolescent in middle school can be growing a degree of connection and relationships with their classmates (increasing their sense of belonging) and increasing their level of personal self-esteem (which is influenced by how they feel they are viewed by—and feel valued by—their peers) while also being hungry or in danger at home.

As deficiency needs, such as acquiring that sense of belonging, become increasingly satisfied, a student is better positioned to experience self-actualization, which stems from a desire to grow. For example, the more adept a high school student becomes at social problem solving in their relationships with their peers, the more likely they will maintain and apply their problem-solving skills over time to new situations. In a sense, the student accrues positive momentum that enhances their journey toward self-actualization while at the same time becoming increasingly resilient. The journey of a student experiencing mental health challenges may appear different on the surface, but the trek toward self-actualization is shared among all of us.

> Systematically embedding trauma-informed approaches within the daily ebb and flow of both classroom and nonclassroom settings, along with such already established programs as mentioned previously, can lower the risk of trauma and other ACEs from emerging in the first place. Embedding trauma-informed approaches can also help mitigate the associated effects of mental health challenges.

HOW CAN MASLOW'S HIERARCHY GUIDE MY TEACHING?

You can frame the way you address the needs of your students within this hierarchy, in which movement is both dynamic and fluid. Rarely will any given student move through the hierarchy in a linear, lockstep manner. Rather, movement is dynamic, just like life. A student may move back and forth among the levels within the hierarchy depending on different situations they experience. In other words, life is dynamic, complicated, and at times messy.

Unfortunately, when deficiency needs become persistent and chronic, progress can be inhibited. Life experiences, such as exposure to ACEs and trauma leading to mental health challenges, can adversely impact a student's ability to navigate the typical school day, let alone the usual stressors that surface throughout the school day. Based on their degree of resiliency associated with the protective factors in their lives, some students may be able to work through difficult school experiences with a modest level of support and understanding from you and your colleagues. Others, such as those experiencing significant mental health challenges, may likely require additional support.

So, what does all this mean to you as an educator when supporting a student who is experiencing mental health challenges? Although not exhaustive by any means, here are a few essential points to keep front and center in your mind:

1. Student growth and development are dynamic, not static. One essential role you play with your students is that you are positioned to become a protective factor in their lives.

2. The presence of a mental health challenge (including, but not limited to, a diagnosed mental illness such as an anxiety or mood disorder) does not fundamentally alter a student's basic human needs as framed within Maslow's hierarchy.

3. As important as competent lesson planning and delivery of instruction is (and it is essential, make no mistake), establishing rapport and connection with your students and encouraging each of them to develop positive relationships with one another is also essential, and it can be particularly critical for a student experiencing mental health challenges.

Relationships and connections serve as the bedrock of protective factors for students who have experienced trauma. As highlighted in Chapter 3, protective factors can make all the difference in the world and can actually help save lives.

ARE MENTAL HEALTH CHALLENGES ON THE RISE?

> Relationships and connections serve as the bedrock of protective factors for students who have experienced trauma.

Concerns about youth mental health have been on the rise for a number of years, even prior to the pandemic. According to the CDC, suicide is the second leading cause of death for individuals between 15 and 24 years of age (CDC, 2021). According to the National Alliance on Mental Illness (NAMI), more than half of individuals experiencing mood disorders struggle to receive treatment in any given year, with access and utilization of mental health treatment for youth particularly challenging (NAMI, 2021). An estimated 1 in 5 children in the U.S. experience mental, emotional, or behavior disorders, including anxiety and depression, each year, but only about 20% receive any form of specialized mental health treatment (CDC, 2021). Schools, and educators such as you, have in many ways become de facto mental health providers for many of our nation's youth.

Here is an equally concerning statistic: Most mental disorders that are diagnosed later in life more often begin by the age of 14 (CDC, 2021). Particular groups of disorders, such as anxiety disorders have been surfacing increasingly and occurring at younger ages. Currently, the median ages of onset for anxiety and mood disorders are 6 and 13 years of age, respectively. Anxiety and major depressive disorders in children and adolescents, as well as deaths by suicide, have been rising at alarming rates for a number of years.

Given these elevated concerns about youth mental health, the importance of trauma-informed practice in the classroom is clear. To paraphrase one anonymous teacher:

> It's not that my kids aren't capable of learning math, it is just all of the other stuff that gets in the way of them being able to focus on learning math. I haven't found a way to effectively lesson plan my way around the growing numbers of my students who share with me how overwhelmed they feel with either anxiety or feelings of sadness and depression.

Implementation of the universal approaches outlined in previous chapters will go a long way toward creating a conducive learning environment for all students, including those students experiencing mental health challenges. In many ways, operating a trauma-informed classroom can serve as a first layer, or universal tier, of youth suicide prevention. To paraphrase the statements by a few survivors of suicide, people do not want to die by suicide, they simply want their pain to end and they see little to no hope for the future (Quinnett, 1995). According to the National Council for Mental Wellbeing, having at least one caring, healthy relationship with a trusted adult may be the single most important protective factor to minimize the risk of youth suicide (Swarbrick & Brown, 2013). As a teacher, you may be that one caring adult for one or more of your students.

Trauma-informed approaches support the healthy social and emotional growth and development of our students. As the old adage goes, an ounce of prevention is worth a pound of cure. Lowering the risk for suicidal thoughts or actions of your students is greatly enhanced through utilization of the trauma-informed approaches highlighted throughout this book.

As noted previously, some of your students will likely require additional services and supports layered on top of the universal trauma-informed classroom strategies described so far. In many instances, these services and supports will require a team approach. Different aspects of targeted or individual-intensive services may be provided by mental health professionals in collaboration with educational services provided in your classroom, in the school, or in the local community. Chapter 11, while not the primary emphasis of this book, delves into addressing the needs of students who require targeted or individual-intensive supports, those at the Tier 3 level.

REFLECTIVE EXERCISE

The most important protective factors that exist for students experiencing mental health challenges are feeling connected and having trusting relationships. Think about a student of concern who comes to mind when you think about applying a trauma-informed lens. Once you have identified the student, reflect on what you have learned in this and previous chapters, and complete the final column in Figure 10.2 in relevant domains concerning _____ (your focus student).

Targeted connections and relationships to facilitate	Facilitation strategies to implement
With me	Me:
With other school staff	Other school staff:
With classmates	Classmates:
With other school peers	Other school peers:
With others in the community	Others in the community:
With other family members	Other family members:

Figure 10.2. Reflective exercise on relationship facilitation.

11

Trauma-Informed Multi-Tiered Systems of Support

Trauma-informed practices are best viewed through the lens or framework of MTSS (see Figure 3.1). Equally applicable across all school systems and relevant to meeting the needs of all students, such practices are promoted by federally funded initiatives (Figure 11.1).

The trauma-informed practices highlighted in the chapters to this point reflect universal preventive (Tier 1) approaches. These preventive strategies are within your direct sphere of influence and will help you meet the needs of most of your students, but there will likely be some students who require targeted, or perhaps even individual-intensive, supports. Let's start by identifying targeted (Tier 2) approaches that can be layered on top of the universal approaches you use in your classroom.

WHAT IS INVOLVED IN TIER 2 APPROACHES?

One of the hallmarks of both advanced tier approaches is the increased use of progress monitoring to further identify the student's needs along with patterns and potential functions of concerning behavior. This occurs in tandem with identification of environmental factors that adversely influence the student's growth and their behaviors coupled with establishment of procedures to modify interventions and supports. These advanced tier supports also simultaneously involve increasing precision as well as frequency in use of each component of REAP (e.g., increased rapport building, further clarification of expectations reflecting SEL, increased frequency of positive acknowledgment as well as OTRs) throughout the school day and ideally in home and community settings. Engagement of others to support implementation of support strategies is yet another common feature of a Tier 2 approach. Additional guidance on advanced tier supports appears in Appendices J–M.

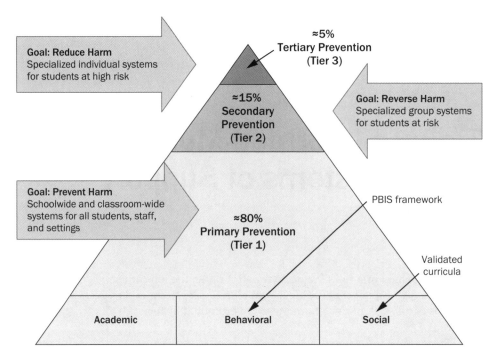

Figure 11.1. Comprehensive, integrated, three-tiered model of prevention. (*Sources:* Lane, Kalberg, & Menzies [2009]; Lane, Oakes, Jenkins, Menzies, & Kalberg [2014].) (*Key:* PBIS, positive behavioral interventions and supports.)

One of the hallmarks of both advanced tier approaches is the increased use of progress monitoring to further identify the student's needs along with patterns and potential functions of concerning behavior. This occurs in tandem with identification of environmental factors that adversely influence the student's growth and their behaviors coupled with establishment of procedures to modify interventions and supports.

There are a variety of Tier 2 interventions and supports to consider. Think of these as a menu of options that to varying degrees will require collaboration with others. One of the more commonly used targeted approaches is behavior contracting. Although a behavior contract can be designed with the student and implemented by you in the classroom, collaboration with others who interact with the student of concern should occur to enhance continuity of delivery across settings and staff.

A second example of a targeted approach commonly implemented in schools is known as Check & Connect (Sinclair et al., 1998). An identified staff member (usually not the classroom teacher) serves as a primary point of contact for the student of concern. Thoughtful consideration as to which staff member should serve in this role is highly encouraged to ensure the best fit. This person's important duties typically include meeting with the student on a periodic basis, as well as serving as a liaison among people including the student and members of their family, school staff, and community supporters.

Schools implementing Check & Connect typically establish two levels of operations within this approach:

- **Basic.** The basic level features the assigned staff member meeting with the student on an infrequent basis (perhaps once a month).

- **Intensive.** At the intensive level, meetings and interactions are more frequent.

Meetings typically focus on progress updates on school performance and the application of problem-solving approaches. Direct review and reteaching of social skills are commonly a part of this approach.

Another Tier 2 approach often used in schools is the Behavior Education Program (Crone et al., 2004), also known as Check-In Check-Out (CICO). Most schools implementing CICO identify a common staff member (often a paraprofessional) with whom targeted students check in at the start of the school day and check out at the end of the day (or, in some instances, a.m. and p.m. check-in and check-out, respectively).

- **Check-in meetings.** These usually focus on preparedness for the school day, including homework and materials checks and a behavior progress report/daily progress report (DPR) that the student presents to their teachers on entry to each classroom throughout the day.

- **Check-out meetings.** These involve tallying the daily points earned by the student and delivery of contingent reinforcement for hitting a target.

An additional Tier 2 approach often used in schools is targeted social skills training. In many instances, students are scheduled for reteaching activities associated with the established behavioral expectations reflecting SEL. This brings together those students who appear to need additional instruction and feedback in social skills for supplemental instruction in a nonpunitive manner. Reteaching usually occurs in small-group settings and may be provided by an array of staff including teachers, guidance counselors, and school social workers. The reteaching sessions may be organized in a variety of ways. You may have direct involvement in delivering these additional small-group remedial sessions, or you may not. At a minimum, as the classroom teacher, you should be in the loop and provide guidance and feedback about the student(s) of concern on an ongoing basis, as well as reinforce targeted social skills taught during reteaching sessions throughout the day as appropriate.

Mentoring is yet another Tier 2 approach that has been implemented successfully in school settings. Throughout this book, we have emphasized the importance of relationships, which are also essential to the Tier 2 strategies highlighted here. The foundation of mentoring is in fostering connectedness within the school (and, in an extended sense, with the community). Depending on how the program is designed and implemented, mentoring tends to foster more naturally occurring student support systems.

All of these Tier 2 strategies can prove helpful and are typically within the wheelhouse of most schools. However, we cannot emphasize enough that a team approach is highly recommended in selecting, organizing, and providing targeted strategies. The approaches must be matched to student needs, implemented with fidelity, and assessed on a regular basis to measure their impact.

HOW DO TIER 2 STRATEGIES ALIGN WITH MENTAL HEALTH SERVICES?

Tier 2 approaches can have even greater impact when aligned with mental health services that support students with mental disorders. Depending on the school system, mental health services may be provided face-to-face or virtually on school grounds or in community-based settings. The delivery of mental health services should be aligned with the student assistance program in operation in your school, and it must be thoughtfully coordinated with other services (e.g., special education programming) when relevant.

A vast array of targeted mental health treatments may be provided by qualified mental health providers and aligned and coordinated with Tier 2 supports provided by the school. These are based, of course, on the unique needs of the student. A few examples of such programs are highlighted in Table 11.1.

Table 11.1.   Examples of targeted mental health treatment programs

Aggression Replacement Training (ART) (Glick & Goldstein, 1987)	Cognitive Behavioral Intervention for Trauma in Schools (CBITS) (Jaycox, 2004)	The BLUES Program (Stice et al., 2008)
ART is a cognitive-behavioral intervention for reduction of aggressive and violent behavior that originally focused on adolescents. This multimodal program has three components: 1) Social Skills, 2) Anger Control Training, and 3) Moral Reasoning. ART was developed in the United States in the 1980s by Arnold P. Goldstein and Barry Glick and is now used throughout the country in human service systems, including juvenile justice systems, schools, and adult corrections. Each of the three components uses a process to ensure that youth learn the skills in class and transfer them to new situations outside of the group. The approach emphasizes Piaget's concept of peer learning and reflects the belief that youth learn best from other youth.	CBITS is a school-based group intervention (for Grades 5–12) that has been shown to reduce posttraumatic stress disorder and depression symptoms and psychosocial dysfunction in children who have experienced trauma. Bounce Back is an adaptation of CBITS for elementary school students (Grades K–5). The linkages among trauma exposure, physical health, behavioral health, and academic functioning underscore the importance of integrating trauma-informed care within educational settings for students in need of this level of targeted support.	The BLUES Program, developed by Paul Rohde and Eric Stice at the Oregon Research Institute, actively engages high school students with depressive symptoms or those at risk of onset of major depression. The approach includes six weekly 1-hour group sessions and home practice assignments. Weekly sessions focus on building group rapport and increasing participant involvement in pleasant activities (all sessions), learning and practicing cognitive restructuring techniques (Sessions 2–4), and developing response plans to future life stressors (Sessions 5–6). In-session exercises require participants to apply skills taught in the program. Home practice assignments are intended to reinforce the skills taught in the sessions and help participants learn how to apply these skills to their daily life.

WHAT ELSE CAN BE DONE IF TIER 2 APPROACHES
LAYERED ON TOP OF MY TIER 1 APPROACHES ARE NOT ENOUGH?

Don't worry—all is not lost, by any means. In fact, all of your efforts thus far have set the stage for layering on Tier 3 (individual-intensive) approaches. Before going into detail, you need to have a basic understanding of individual-intensive interventions and supports. The development and implementation of individual-intensive approaches that are effective, sustainable, and student centered requires a team approach. This bears repeating yet again: A team approach is absolutely necessary to achieve meaningful outcomes that can endure over time.

> The development and implementation of individual-intensive approaches that are effective, sustainable, and student centered requires a team approach.

It is important to keep things in perspective. One of the keys to providing effective Tier 3 supports is an understanding of two interrelated processes:

1. Decoding why the student engages in the behaviors of concern

2. Layering on specific strategies that align with assessment results

Decoding student behavior (Point 1) sets the stage for providing specific interventions and supports with measurable results. An FBA is an information-gathering process that can help your team understand the reasons for the student's behavior. This is the same FBA process required by the Individuals with Disabilities Education Improvement Act (IDEA) of 2004 (PL 108-446). Numerous published resources are available should your team need to conduct a comprehensive FBA.

The FBA process involves asking a series of questions and capturing information (data) relevant to your responses in order to form an educated guess (hypothesis) as to the nature of the student's needs and behavior. This information is then discussed among members of your team. Keep in mind that your concern may be about externalizing behaviors and/or underlying internalized conditions. If you can predict when the behavior of concern is likely to occur, you are in a better position to identify and address the causal root, or function, of the behavior. If it turns out that the causal root does not lend itself to being addressed completely, decoding can still help mitigate adverse effects by identifying triggers and designing and implementing an individualized positive behavior support plan (PBSP).

In Chapter 2, you learned how to apply a general functional lens to student behavior in your classroom. Let's build on that approach in terms of Tier 3 supports. Decoding the triggers (antecedents) as well as the function(s) of a given student's behavior makes the selection and implementation of interventions and supports a logical, systematic process. Creating hypotheses about the causes of concerning behavior minimizes the degree of random trial and error on your part and can help you elicit the desired behavior change in the most time-efficient way possible. Table 11.2 provides some examples of specific functions of student problem behavior along with common consequences and related

> Decoding the function(s) of a given student's behavior makes the selection and implementation of interventions and supports a logical, systematic process.

Table 11.2. Examples of common consequences associated with specific functions

Function	Common consequences	Trauma-informed considerations
To **escape (avoid):** After a behavior occurs, the student avoids something unpleasant or terminates a situation that they perceive as unpleasurable.	The teacher provides assistance to make the task easier. The student gets out of doing the task. Use of time-out for problem behavior increases. Performance demands are lessened. Adults stop "nagging." Peers stop teasing. The student is left alone.	It is natural for a student to engage in actions to avoid or escape triggering events that they find painful. A triggering event to a student experiencing trauma may not be perceived by others as painful or even out of the norm.
To **get something** (access to social interaction, preferred objects or events of sensory stimulation or calm): After a behavior occurs, the student gets something that they desire.	The student gets one-to-one teacher interaction, or teacher contact increases. The teacher verbally responds (even neutral or negative comments may be desired by the student). Peers respond by laughing. Student gets more intense reactions. The student is redirected to a more preferred activity. The student gains access to things they want (e.g., objects, activities, other students). The student gets enjoyment or feels good as a result of engaging in the behavior (e.g., sensory stimulation).	Many students who have experienced trauma understandably act in ways to address their needs for safety, sustenance, a sense of belonging, and self-esteem. The key to supporting students who have experienced trauma is not trying to alter the need, but rather engineering environments to minimize exposure to triggers in concert with teaching habilitative ways for the student to address their needs.

trauma-informed considerations. When patterns emerge, consider the implications of trauma that may have been, or is perhaps currently being, experienced. The key to supporting students who have experienced trauma is not trying to alter the need, but rather engineering environments to minimize exposure to triggers and teaching positive ways for the student to address their needs.

The examples included in Table 11.2 are just that—examples. Please do not misinterpret or overgeneralize these illustrations. It is also important to remember that a given behavior of concern by any particular student does not always serve the same function in all situations. Determining the function of a given student's behavior should instead be the result of a student-centered FBA that assesses the student's behavior in context. It is only by asking a core set of FBA questions within a team-based approach that you can effectively decode the nature of a particular student's behavior.

FBAs have been known to create a lot of stress for educators in the field, especially when an effective team structure for collaboration is challenging to access.

Compounding this sense of angst is the format of FBAs. They are often written to address legal requirements associated with special education under IDEA 2004, or to align with professional journals, which more typically present empirical (scientific) studies concerning students with extreme forms of serious problem behavior. These aspects of FBAs are important but unfortunately can hinder their translation to establishing common, everyday applications in typical school settings.

WHAT ARE THE BASICS OF CONDUCTING AN INITIAL (ENTRY-LEVEL) FUNCTIONAL BEHAVIORAL ASSESSMENT?

At its very root, an FBA is nothing more than a problem-solving process. It addresses a series of core questions regarding a given student and their behavior in the context of their life circumstances and environments. You can gather information (collect data) in many different ways when conducting an FBA (which has to some extent added to the degree of confusion in the field). Given the array of information-gathering procedures available, it can become difficult sometimes to see the forest (the FBA) because of all the trees (potential data-collection processes).

We have found that teams are best able to understand the FBA process by connecting the core questions to familiar practices within their classrooms. For example, think about the basic approach to teaching reading in your classroom. Regardless of whether you are teaching young children to read for comprehension or high school students to read a textbook for understanding, you encourage them to think about key questions as they read. Guiding your students to ask the infamous five *Wh-* questions—*who, what, when, where,* and *why*—when reading is one commonly accepted approach. This process also has relevance for a team conducting an FBA. In essence, conducting an initial (entry-level) FBA with a given student involves asking this same series of *Wh-* questions, with an emphasis on the student's behavior and its context. Table 11.3 presents a series of general decoding *Wh-* questions to ask concerning a student named "Jimmy," who was exhibiting what his team initially documented as disruptive behavior, along with some trauma-informed considerations.

The reason for asking these questions is to help gain an understanding as to why the student, Jimmy in this case, engages in the behavior of concern. Insight can help your team select prevention and intervention approaches that are compatible with your approach to classroom operations to address the student's needs. At a conceptual level, an FBA helps you to decode the series of events involved in problem behavior and decipher how each of those events is related to the others in the A-B-C chain.

The primary purposes for conducting an FBA are to prevent problem behaviors by identifying relevant strategies and supports to address the student's needs, to teach socially appropriate skills, and to provide logical humane consequences for both desired and undesired behaviors. An FBA should result in a PBSP that reflects a healthy balance of prevention, teaching, and consequences (keep in mind the 80%/20% balance we previously described) .

The development and implementation of a multicomponent PBSP for an individual student is an important—and necessary—aspect of providing individual-intensive (Tier 3) approaches. The key to designing appropriate interventions and supports is to use your team's hypotheses as a navigational tool.

Table 11.3.   Logical general decoding *Wh-* questions and trauma-informed considerations

A-B-C component	General decoding *Wh-* questions	Further trauma-informed questions
Antecedent (context)	**Who** is Jimmy with when he becomes disruptive? **When** is Jimmy's disruptive behavior most likely to occur? **What** circumstances make misbehavior more likely? **When** is Jimmy's disruptive behavior least likely to occur? **What** is the nature of the routines and settings in which Jimmy acts appropriately?	Has Jimmy been exposed to particular adverse childhood experiences or traumatic events that are possibly impacting his behavior? From Jimmy's perspective, what associations exist between triggering events in the environment and his trauma experiences?
Behavior	**What** exactly does Jimmy do that is a problem? **What** does Jimmy look like and sound like when he is disruptive? **When** is Jimmy's behavior occurring (how often, frequency), or how long, (duration), or how intensely (magnitude)?	How immediately or imminently harmful is the behavior of concern to Jimmy, to others, and to the environment?
Consequence (function)	**Why** does Jimmy engage in the problem behavior? **What** does he get or avoid as a result of being disruptive (what is the payoff for Jimmy)?	Does the behavior help Jimmy avoid/escape events that he associates with trauma? Does the behavior help Jimmy satisfy deprivation-type needs (e.g., safety, sustenance, belonging, self-esteem) in part or as a whole?

> The development and implementation of a multicomponent PBSP for an individual student is an important—and necessary—aspect of providing individual-intensive (Tier 3) approaches.

Make sure that the interventions and supports identified in the student's PBSP are linked clearly with both the triggers of the student's behavior and its function(s). As already noted, we provide some guidance in the appendices to help link your team's FBA results (hypotheses) with the selection of interventions and supports for a student-centered PBSP (see Appendices M–P). We also provide some guidance to help your team with implementation of a multicomponent support plan (see Appendix Q).

HOW CAN A TRAUMA-INFORMED APPROACH HELP WITH TIER 3 SUPPORT?

Even in this day and age, conducting an FBA and then designing and implementing a multicomponent PBSP is something with which many school-based teams continue to struggle. Trauma-informed considerations can be factored in to enhance this type of Tier 3 support. Implementation of a PBSP can be greatly enhanced when aligned with person-centered planning processes, such as Personal Futures Planning (Mount, 1994), Essential Lifestyle Planning (Smull & Sanderson, 2009), and

RENEW (Rehabilitation for Empowerment, Natural Supports, Education, and Work; Malloy et al., 2010).

When supporting students experiencing mental disorders, Tier 3 supports should be aligned with mental health services when relevant. As was the case with Tier 2 supports, mental health services can be provided face-to-face or virtually on school grounds or in community-based settings. The delivery of mental health services should align with student assistance programs available at school and other services (e.g., special education programming) when relevant.

> Most targeted supports, and most certainly all forms of individual-intensive supports, require collaborative teaming with respect to both design and implementation.

As described for Tier 2 support, there is a vast array of mental health treatment programs relevant to Tier 3 support that may be provided to students by qualified mental health providers and aligned with a PBSP. A few examples of such programs are highlighted in Table 11.4.

The design and delivery of advanced tier supports to students reflect increasing degrees of labor intensity and precision. Most targeted supports, and most certainly all forms of individual-intensive supports, require collaborative teaming with respect to both design and implementation.

Sound implementation of the universal preventive approaches highlighted in this book (think back to our REAP mnemonic) can help reduce or mitigate the risk factors that can lead to the need for more labor-intensive supports. However, you will likely encounter at least a small number of students who require advanced-tier supports.

Table 11.4. Examples of mental health treatment programs that can be aligned with a positive behavior support plan

Cognitive-Behavioral Therapy (CBT)	Dialectical Behavioral Therapy (DBT)	Eye Movement Desensitization and Reprocessing (EMDR)
CBT is a broad range of psychotherapeutic methods or psychotherapies to help clients overcome dysfunctional thought patterns and behavior patterns. Because all forms of CBT are based on the idea that thoughts primarily affect emotions and actions, CBT focuses on changing and controlling the way individuals deal with their thoughts.	DBT is one form of CBT. Originally developed by Marsha M. Linehan for the treatment of personality disorders, it has since been successfully adapted for use with other mental health disorders that stem from problems with emotional regulation, such as eating disorders and bipolar disorder. From a position of nonjudgmental acceptance and validation of their feelings, this therapy helps individuals cope with out-of-control emotions by using a set of four practical skills: 1) how to be more effective in interpersonal relationships, 2) how to tolerate and accept distressing situations more easily, 3) how to regulate emotions, and 4) how to use mindfulness-based skills to accomplish any of the preceding tasks.	EMDR is a form of psychotherapy developed by Francine Shapiro in the 1990s. The person being treated is asked to recall distressing images; the therapist then directs them in one of a number of types of bilateral sensory input, such as side-to-side eye movements or hand tapping. EMDR is included in several evidence-based guidelines for the treatment of posttraumatic stress disorder.

Sound implementation of REAP will help you create a climate in your classroom that is more conducive to providing advanced-tier supports when needed. In other words, implementation of REAP can help build student resiliency and may reduce the need for advanced-tier supports in the first place. However, if advanced-tier supports are needed, expansion and enhancement of your implementation of the REAP components should be reflected in those advanced-tier supports. Further, as a result of your reading this book, you and your colleagues now have an understanding of the necessary tools and trauma-informed approaches to help you address even the most challenging levels of student need.

REFLECTIVE EXERCISE

Think about your experiences with your past students for this reflective exercise. Specifically, hone in on one of those students who presented the greatest degree of complex needs. Note some of those most challenging needs in the left-hand column of Figure 11.2. In the middle column, provide examples of the interventions and supports that were designed to meet those needs. In the final column, identify to what degree the identified REAP component was implemented with success. Focus specifically in this third column on answering the following questions: 1) Was the expanded/enhanced component a prominent feature in what was provided? 2) If it was a prominent feature, to what degree was it provided with integrity and consistency? and 3) If it was implemented with integrity and consistency, were meaningful student growth and progress realized?

Targeted student's needs	Interventions & supports provided	Presence/Degree/Success of REAP component
		Targeted increased rapport building:
		Further clarity of expectations with SEL:
		Increased frequency of positive reinforcement:
		Increased infusion of OTRs:

Figure 11.2.   Reflective exercise on complex support needs. (*Key:* OTRs, opportunities to respond; SEL, social and emotional learning.)

Closing Thoughts on Self-Care

Our hunch is that you have likely flown on a plane to a targeted destination at some point in time in the not-too-distant past. Recall that, just prior to take-off, the flight attendants review "important safety information." One of the final pieces of advice they provide to passengers is what to do if the cabin loses sufficient oxygen levels for breathing, triggering the masks to drop down. They tell you to always put on your own oxygen mask before trying to help someone else with theirs. The reason they suggest this is, of course, to increase the likelihood that you are part of the solution rather than someone who becomes in need of help.

Self-care reflects this exact same principle. In contrast to the plane analogy, we suggest that you think of self-care proactively rather than in response to a crisis. This will allow you to become increasingly resilient over time and should reduce the chances of succumbing to *compassion fatigue* (extreme tiredness and desperation experienced as an outgrowth of working day in and day out with students navigating trauma in their lives). If left unchecked, compassion fatigue can lead to burnout, hindering your resiliency and decreasing your effectiveness at school and in your personal life.

There are many different ways to practice self-care, and no "one size fits all." Self-care includes self-awareness; you must be aware of your own level of resiliency across situations and time needed to navigate the stressors in your life in order to best help your students increase their resiliency. Knowing when to reach out for help is a necessary skill, as well as a strength, when feeling like you are approaching your wits' end.

The takeaways here are 1) acknowledging the need to practice self-care, 2) identifying time-efficient self-care strategies that work for you, and 3) investing time in implementing strategies that are a good fit for you in a proactive manner. After reflecting on a variety of self-care resources available through search engines, review Table C.1, which highlights five essential self-care strategies that we suggest are worthy of consideration.

Our goal in providing these closing thoughts is not to add to the burden of resources available to you as an educator. Instead, our goal is to highlight the importance of self-care, especially when using a trauma-informed approach to help vulnerable students, and to provide some initial guidance for how to go about it. A few resources that highlight self-care using a more structured approach are noted here and included in the Resources for Further Guidance for your convenience and possible exploration. We wish you good luck!

Table C.1.   Self-care strategies for teachers

Strategy	Examples and illustrations
Engage in activities you enjoy.	Examples include physical activities (e.g., hiking, biking outdoors, yoga) as well as more sedentary endeavors (e.g., curling up with a good book or watching a favorite show on TV). The key is to hone in on what you enjoy doing and then build it into the ebb and flow of your activities. If you set goals associated with new activities, such as working out, make sure they are realistic so you can experience success and gain momentum. Another practice is an attitude of gratitude: periodic reflection on positive and joyful moments through meditation, conversation with others, or journaling.
Spend time with people you enjoy.	As we all know, relationships are essential. Make time to reach out and connect with friends and acquaintances. Much like a bank account, the more you invest in relationships over time, the more "currency" you build up. That way, if you "hit the wall" in any sense, you have that currency more readily available to spend when you need help.
Establish and maintain healthy habits.	Be sure to get enough physical activity, eat healthfully, and get sufficient sleep each day. Find what fills your "tank" with sufficient energy to allow you to focus and self-regulate your own actions. Regarding physical activity, some people are well-suited to vigorous exercise, whereas others might need something less strenuous. The key is to find your "sweet spot" and build the activity into your daily routine until it becomes a habit. The same goes for sleeping and diet (within reason of course—an occasional late night or sweet treat is okay). Exploring mindfulness activities is another healthy habit that can help you to become even more grounded and resilient.
Get support when you need it—*before* crisis.	Personal resiliency is dynamic, not static. It can change across situations and over time. Be aware of your limitations and stay tuned in to indicators that you may be approaching your personal threshold *before* you actually reach it. Think of this as an advanced warning system like the indicator lights on a car's dashboard. Be aware of your own personal indicator lights, and if any of them flash a warning sign, respond. Resources available to you through work (e.g., employee assistance programs) and personal relationships (e.g., a friend or colleague who can help you seek professional help if you need it) can help you turn off those indicator lights. Add to your cell phone contacts the number for Crisis Text Line (741-741) and/or other help lines (e.g., dial 988 to connect with the National Suicide Prevention Hotline). Remember, asking for help when you need it is a sign of strength, not weakness!
Make time—actually schedule it—to relax.	Simply stated, unplug when you can. Between emails and social media, the level of noise that exists in all of our lives can be deafening. Establish boundaries with respect to initiating and responding to emails. When it comes to social media, be conscious of your patterns of use. Habits—both good and bad—form, almost subconsciously over time, the more you engage in them. Think about whether your social media use is a good habit or a bad habit. Be aware of your patterns of usage and self-regulate. There is an array of available strategies to help you change your pattern of usage. Seek help if you need it.

RESOURCES FOR FURTHER GUIDANCE

- *WISE Teacher Well-Being Workbook*
  - Developed by Georgetown University Hospital staff and the National Center for School Mental Health, this workbook is designed to assist you in developing a personal well-being plan.
  - Resources by MedStar Georgetown Center for Wellbeing in School Environments website: https://www.medstarwise.org/resources
  - Workbook: https://static1.squarespace.com/static/60411ac3e851e139836af5f1/t/6155e14e69ae5761df34cfe0/1633018213269/TeacherWISE_9.30.21-web.pdf

- *Onward: Cultivating Emotional Resilience in Educators* and *The Onward Workbook: Daily Activities to Cultivate Your Emotional Resilience and Thrive*
  - Both of the following resources were developed by Elena Aguilar and provide structured guidance to build emotional resilience (Companion website: https://www.onwardthebook.com/resources/):
    - Aguilar, E. (2018). *Onward: Cultivating emotional resilience in educators.* John Wiley. https://10.1002/9781119441731
    - Aguilar, E. (2018). *The Onward Workbook: Daily activities to cultivate your emotional resilience and thrive.* Jossey-Bass. https://10.1002/9781119441779

- **University at Buffalo's School of Social Work: Self-Care Starter Kit**
  - Initially developed for social work students in training, the integrated self-paced resources have been used across disciplines and in the professional field. It is recommended to start with *Introduction to Self-Care,* followed by *Developing Your Self-Care Plan* modules.
  - Website: https://socialwork.buffalo.edu/resources/self-care-starter-kit.html

Appendices

The Three Bees (Elementary School)

Expectation	Arrival at school	Individual work	Teacher talking	Group activities	Changing activities
Be Ready	• Go immediately to your classroom after arriving at school. • Bring your homework with you to class. • Be in your seat when the morning bell rings.	• Have your materials open and on top of your desk. • Follow directions the first time. • Get to work right away.	• Listen when Mrs. Lee speaks; one person speaks at a time. • Write important things in your notebook.	• Be focused on the group work to be completed. • Have your materials with you and opened to the assigned page. • Organize your group and get to work quickly (within 1 min).	• Be aware of the daily schedule. • Listen for directions from Mrs. Lee. • Be flexible in case the schedule changes.
Be Responsible	• Be on time to school and class. • Listen when Mrs. Lee speaks; one person speaks at a time. • Have homework. • Use indoor voices when speaking.	• Follow directions on tests and assignments. • Organize and get to work promptly. • Make a good effort on all work. • Speak only at appropriate times.	• Think about what Mrs. Lee says. • Ask Mrs. Lee questions by raising your hand. • Volunteer to answer questions by raising your hand.	• All contribute. • One person speaks at a time using indoor voice. • Ask for help as needed. Finish on time. • Share with others while keeping your hands and feet to yourself.	• Stop and put things away when Mrs. Lee says to do so. • Know what materials you need for next class/activity. • Keep your hands and feet to yourself. • Use indoor voices when speaking.
Be Respectful	• Say "hi" to friends before homeroom starts. • Keep hands and feet to yourself. • Listen when Mrs. Lee speaks; one person speaks at a time. • Follow directions the first time.	• Get to work and work quietly. • Use only your materials. • Ask for help by raising your hand. • Make a good effort.	• Listen and follow directions the first time. • Think about what Mrs. Lee is saying. • Ask questions by raising your hand. • Volunteer to answer questions by raising your hand.	• Encourage others to work cooperatively. • Keep hands and feet to yourself. • It is okay to disagree, but do it without being disagreeable. • Be thoughtful of others.	• Be thoughtful of others. • Keep hands and feet to yourself. • Use indoor voices. • When moving in a room or hallway, always walk on the right side.

Expected Behavior (Middle School)

Expectation	Start of class	Individual work	Teacher lecture	Group work	End of class
Be on time and prepared.	• Arrive on time to class. • Bring your notebook and writing materials. • Listen when Mrs. Jones starts class (only one person speaks at a time).	• Be focused on your work and ignore distractions. • Remember to follow procedures for all individual assignments. • Organize your work and get to work quickly after directed by Mrs. Jones.	• Be focused on the current unit of instruction. • Use your notebook for taking notes. • Please listen and follow along when Mrs. Jones is speaking (only one person speaks at a time).	• Be focused on the task to be completed. • Have your notebook opened to the proper section being covered. • Organize as a team quickly and start work promptly (within 1 min).	• Adequately prepare materials to leave the classroom (e.g., place only your materials in your backpack). • Travel to your next classroom promptly when dismissed by Mrs. Jones.
Be responsible for your actions.	• Arrive on time to class. • Listen when Mrs. Jones starts class (only one person speaks at a time). • Come prepared by completing all assignments and readings. • Follow all directions provided by Mrs. Jones as you enter the room.	• Remember to follow procedures for individual work. • Organize and do the best work that you can, even on a bad day. • Control your actions and make your time productive.	• Listen and think about points raised in Mrs. Jones's comments. • Ask questions of Mrs. Jones and respond to questions. • Gain attention by raising your hand; be patient.	• Make sure everyone has an opportunity to contribute. • One person speaks at a time. • Ask for help as needed. • Successfully complete task within allotted time frame. • Share roles on the team (e.g., recorder/timekeeper/ notetaker).	• Be sure you have written down all assignments to be completed prior to your next class. • Leave classroom in the same condition you found it when you arrived.
Be respectful toward others.	• Say "hello" to others using appropriate voice and language before class starts. • Listen when Mrs. Jones starts class (only one person speaks at a time). • Help others if asked for help.	• Get to work quickly on individual work. • Be on task and work quietly. • Raise your hand to get Mrs. Jones's attention.	• Please follow along when Mrs. Jones is speaking (only one person speaks at a time). • Think about what Mrs. Jones is saying.	• Encourage others to be on task. • Organize as a team quickly and start work promptly (within 1 min). • Strive for consensus whenever possible. • Share differences of opinion in a manner that is thoughtful of others.	• Be patient and wait your turn if you need to speak with Mrs. Jones after class. • Leave the room in an orderly manner.

The Teacher's Guide for Effective Classroom Management: A Trauma-Informed Approach, Third Edition
by Tim Knoster and Stephanie Gardner. Copyright © 2024 by Paul H. Brookes Publishing Co., Inc. All rights reserved.

APPENDIX C **Performance Expectations (High School)**

Expectation	Start of class	During individual tests	During lecture in class	During other team activities	Outside of class time preparation
Be here/Be ready. • On time	• Arrive on time to class. • Bring your notebook and writing materials. • Listen when Mr. Smith starts talking (only one person speaks at a time).	• Be focused on the current unit tests. • Remember to follow procedures for individual tests. • Organize and get to work promptly.	• Be focused on the current unit of instruction. • Use your notebook for taking notes. • Please listen and follow along when Mr. Smith is speaking (only one person speaks at a time).	• Be focused on the task to be completed. • Have your notebook opened to the section being covered. • Organize as a team quickly and start work promptly (within 1 min).	• Review prior class notes before next class. • Adequately prepare by doing readings and assignments. • Keep your materials organized.
Be responsible. • Do quality work. • Collaborate.	• Arrive on time to class. • Listen when Mr. Smith starts talking (only one person speaks at a time). • Come prepared by completing all assignments and readings. • Follow procedures in course organizer if you miss a class.	• Remember to follow procedures for individual tests. • Organize and get to work promptly; make a good effort on each question. • Be on task and ask for clarification as needed from Mr. Smith.	• Listen and think about points raised in the lecture. • Ask questions and respond to questions. • Share your perspective on relevant issues on the topic at hand.	• Everyone contributes. • One person speaks at a time. • Ask for help as needed. • Successfully complete task within allotted time frame. • Share roles on the team (e.g., recorder/timekeeper/notetaker).	• Review prior class notes before next class. • Adequately prepare by doing readings and assignments. • Keep your materials organized.
Be respectful. • Encourage others. • Recognize others.	• Politely greet classmates and teacher when arriving to class. • Ask others how things are going. • Listen when Mr. Smith starts talking (only one person speaks at a time). • Provide guidance to classmates who may have been absent from last class.	• Get to work quickly on individual tests. • Be on task and work quietly.	• Please listen and follow along when Mr. Smith is speaking (only one person speaks at a time). • Think about the concepts and practices being described; get the most you can out of the class.	• Encourage others to be on task and to provide their perspective. • Organize as a team quickly and start work promptly (within 1 min). • Strive for consensus whenever possible. • Share differences of opinion in a manner that is thoughtful of others.	• Review prior class notes before next class. • Adequately prepare by doing readings and assignments. • Keep your materials organized.

Expectations Planning Matrix With Embedded Social and Emotional Learning

Expectations	Context 1	Context 2	Context 3	Context 4
Expectation 1				
Expectation 2				
Expectation 3				
Expectation 4				
Expectation 5				

Strategies for Self-Monitoring the 4:1 Ratio in the Classroom

STRATEGY 1

Group: Place 20 paper clips in one pocket and 20 paper clips in another pocket at the start of the day. Remove a paper clip from your right pocket every time you "catch a kid being good" and provide reinforcement to that same child for meeting the behavioral expectations. Remove one paper clip from your left pocket every time you provide behavioral correction to one of your kids during this same day. At the end of the day, tally up how many paper clips you have remaining in your pockets and then calculate a ratio based on your count (e.g., zero paper clips remaining in your right pocket [20 delivered] vs. 15 remaining in your left pocket [five delivered] converts to a 4:1 ratio of positive reinforcement vs. corrective feedback). You may also vary the time interval as you deem appropriate (e.g., 1 hour vs. an entire day).

Individual: Replicate the group process but focus on a given child as warranted.

STRATEGY 2

Group: Loosely wrap a piece of masking tape around your right wrist and your left wrist. Have a marker in your pocket. Place one tally mark on the tape around your right wrist for every time you "catch a kid being good," and provide reinforcement to that same child for meeting the behavioral expectations. Place a tally mark on your left wrist every time you provide behavioral correction to one of your kids during the same day. At the end of the day, tally how many marks you have on your right wrist and on your left wrist, and then calculate a ratio based on your count (e.g., 20 tallies on right wrist vs. five tallies on left wrist converts to a 4:1 ratio of positive reinforcement vs. corrective feedback). You may also vary the time interval as you deem appropriate (e.g., 1 hour vs. an entire day).

Individual: Replicate the group process but focus on a given child as warranted.

Monitoring Achievement of the 4:1 Ratio

Date/time of probe: _____

Student names	Reinforcement received from teacher	Total	Redirection received from teacher	Total	Ratio of + to −
Sample Student	+ + + +	4	−	1	4 to 1
Whole class:					

Student Response Cards

A	**True**	**Agree** 👍
B	**False**	**Disagree** 👎
C	**Yes**	**Increase** ⬆
D	**No**	**Decrease** ⬇

Opportunities to Respond (OTR) Response Sheet

AGREE **DISAGREE**

YES **NO**

A B C D

TRUE FALSE

Opportunities to Respond Data Collection Form (for Teacher Self-Reflection)

Definition of opportunities to respond (OTRs): Teacher behaviors (i.e., the antecedent stimulus) that occasion student responses delivered to one or more students where the student(s) have a chance to respond, and the teacher provides feedback contingent on student responses (MacSuga-Gage & Simonsen, 2015).

Date	Subject/ Skill area	Individual OTR tally	Group/Unison OTR tally	Total OTR	Total time of activity (minutes/seconds)	OTR (per minute)	Methods of OTRs utilized

OTR suggested rates (reflected in the literature)—for reference

Council for Exceptional Children, 1987:

- 4–6 OTRs per minute with new content while looking for 80% accuracy in student responses
- When reviewing materials, increasing the response rate to 8–12 per minute and aiming for a higher accuracy of 90%

Scott et al., 2011:

- At least 3 OTRs per minute with new content as a solid rate to impact student academic and behavioral growth

Behavior Progress Report (Primary Classroom)

Name: _____   Date: _____

☺ = 2 points

😐 = 1 point

☹ = 0 points

Points received: _____   **Points reached:** _____   **Daily goal reached? YES ☐ NO ☐**

Be responsible	Early morning	Late morning	Early afternoon	Late afternoon	Daily total
Keep my hands, feet, body, and objects to myself.	☹ 😐 ☺	☹ 😐 ☺	☹ 😐 ☺	☹ 😐 ☺	☺ = _____ 😐 = _____ ☹ = _____
Say nice things to other people.	☹ 😐 ☺	☹ 😐 ☺	☹ 😐 ☺	☹ 😐 ☺	☺ = _____ 😐 = _____ ☹ = _____
Follow adult directions the first time.	☹ 😐 ☺	☹ 😐 ☺	☹ 😐 ☺	☹ 😐 ☺	☺ = _____ 😐 = _____ ☹ = _____
				Grand total:	☺ = _____ 😐 = _____ ☹ = _____

Behavior Progress Report (Middle or Secondary Classroom)

Student name: _____   Teacher name: _____

2 = Excellent
1 = Satisfactory
0 = Unsatisfactory

Be responsible	Classroom entry/start of class period			Class period until end of class period			Daily total
Keep my hands, feet, body, and objects to myself.	2	1	0	2	1	0	2 = _____ 1 = _____ 0 = _____
Say nice things to other people.	2	1	0	2	1	0	2 = _____ 1 = _____ 0 = _____
Follow adult directions the first time.	2	1	0	2	1	0	2 = _____ 1 = _____ 0 = _____
Date: _____						**Grand Total**	2 = _____ 1 = _____ 0 = _____

Behavior Contract

Student name: _Carl_   Today's date: _10/10/22_

Relevant staff name(s): _John Smith, Jane Goode, Carly Smith, Bob Pevey, Isham Kalou_

Target behavior (behavioral expectation): _Be respectful: Use appropriate language. One person speaks at a time. Listen and follow directions the first time. Speak only at appropriate times. Use an indoor voice when speaking._

Data collection procedure: _Use a good behavior chart with "+" for appropriate and "–" for inappropriate behavior. Teachers and Carl independently evaluate Carl's behavior twice per class period (halfway and at end of each class)._

Reinforcement procedure (what and how often): _Carl can choose from a Choice Box (e.g., box containing homework pass, 10 minutes of extra computer time) at the end of each day when he has earned 7 of 10 "+."_

What must the student do to earn reinforcement? _Be respectful: Use appropriate language. One person speaks at a time. Listen and follow directions the first time. Speak only at appropriate times; use an indoor voice when speaking. 7 of 10 "+" earned each day._

Consequences for failure to meet behavioral expectations: _Carl will not earn access to Choice Box. Other relevant consequences deemed necessary by teacher(s)._

Bonus for exceptional behavioral performance: _When Carl meets expectations 5 consecutive days in a row, he may make a random choice from the Grand Prize Box (e.g., box containing coupons to local sandwich shop, two free movie passes with free popcorn and large drink). When Carl earns two consecutive bonus picks, we will renegotiate the contract._

Signatures of all relevant people: _Carl_   _John Smith_   _Jane Goode_

                                  Carly Smith   _Bob Pevey_   _Isham Kalou_

Guidance for Starting the Conversation About Schoolwide Positive Behavior Intervention and Support (SWPBIS)

- In reality, it is unlikely that there will ever be a "convenient" time to try to initiate a conversation about Schoolwide Positive Behavior Interventions and Supports (PBIS) in a traditional school setting. As such, your degree of success will have less to do with the fact that you have initiated the discussion and more to do with how you go about starting the discussion.

- Contextual factors will have a large impact on how you approach initiating the discussion. For example, you might approach starting the conversation with your building administrator in one way if the administrator has been in the position for many years and has little knowledge of PBIS. However, you may approach getting the conversation started in an entirely different manner if your building administrator is relatively new and/or has (at least some) understanding of PBIS. You will want to carefully think through (analyze) such contextual factors in your planning. In general, it is often most helpful to frame the discussion around whole-school measures of achievement in broaching the topic with building administrators and embedding how your classroom fits into that bigger picture.

- Along these same lines, starting the conversation with your fellow teachers requires some thoughtful planning. Try to identify one or two (or a few) teachers who you feel may be most open to having a conversation about trauma-informed approaches. In general, it is often helpful to frame the discussion around how to enhance student growth and development with your teaching colleagues.

- You may find it helpful to network with teachers in current PBIS schools who themselves have some experience in initiating similar conversations in their respective schools before their schools adopted the PBIS framework. Conferences that focus on positive behavior support (e.g., Association for Positive Behavior Support annual conference) and professional organization and/or project websites emphasizing schoolwide application of positive behavior support (e.g., http:// www.pbis.org) can often help you make such connections if you do not have connections already in place.

Tips for Teaming When Designing and Implementing a Student-Centered Behavior Support Plan

- The process of designing and implementing a student-centered positive behavior support plan (PBSP) requires a team approach that begins with the student and their family and includes educators, other community resources, and support agencies involved with the student.

- As the complexity of the student needs increases, it becomes increasingly important that the team include both sources of natural support (e.g., people from the community) and formal services (staff from other child-serving systems). Teaming within the context of a wraparound process can help provide a holistic approach to service design and delivery, as well as to provide a viable way in which to coordinate services that prioritize meeting the needs of the student within the context of their family and community.

- Acknowledging both the fact that conflict (in the form of differences of opinion) is neither inherently constructive nor destructive and the volatile nature of designing and implementing a PBSP, the team needs to clearly establish basic ground rules for operation that all team members agree to adhere to in order to constructively manage conflict within the team. The team is encouraged, at a minimum, to employ the following ground rules and processes in designing and delivering a PBSP:

  - Agree on use of person- and family-centered processes.

  - Agree on language, avoid jargon, and hold one another accountable.

  - Use people's names in discussions.

  - Agree that only one person speaks at a time.

  - Set clear goals and time frames in each meeting. Also, consider assigning roles at the start of each meeting to help the team function (e.g., timekeeper).

  - Facilitate everyone's involvement in meetings; avoid the situation of a few team members dominating the meeting.

  - Wherever possible, include the student as a member of the team.

  - Periodically discuss at the end of the meetings how the team is functioning.

  - Avoid arguing blindly for positions, avoid statements of absolutes (e.g., "always," "never"), and remember that the focus is on socially valid outcomes.

  - Practice what you preach; support all in expressing their thoughts by remembering the Golden Rule.

  - Be honest.

  - Strive to reach consensus as opposed to simple majority on important matters. All team members need to be able to support the plan in order to achieve sustainable results.

  - Identify a plan facilitator (point person) whenever multiple sources of support will be used (e.g., various child-serving systems, local community members, family members and friends).

  - If or when things go wrong, avoid finger-pointing and casting blame. Address the question "What would it take to make things work better?" when statements like "This isn't working" arise.

  - Focus on strengths and celebrate progress.

Guiding Thoughts for Organizing a
Student-Centered Behavior Support Team

- Designing a comprehensive behavior support plan (BSP) requires a collaborative team approach.

- Student-centered behavior support is a problem-solving process for addressing the support needs of the individual students as well as others involved with the student.

- Student-centered behavior support is assessment based. Interventions and supports are directly linked to environmental influences (inclusive of trauma triggers) and hypotheses concerning the function of the student's behavior of concern.

- Student-centered behavior support usually involves multiple interventions and supports that are provided in a coordinated manner.

- Student-centered behavior support is proactive, emphasizing prevention, by changing the environment and teaching alternative skills.

- Student-centered behavior support is designed for use in everyday settings using typically available resources (the support plan must fit the classroom/school setting).

- Student-centered behavior support holds a broad view of success that includes 1) increases in the acquisition and use of alternative skills, 2) decreases in the incidence of problem behavior, and 3) improvements in quality of life.

- Seek administrative support. Start by discussing the need to develop a student-centered BSP with the building administrator.

- An individualized BSP is likely needed in the following cases. In these cases, establish a team comprising all relevant people involved with the student (people who interact with student regularly and/or who will live with the results of the interventions and supports).

  - The student's undesired behavior persists despite consistently implemented classroom-based interventions.

  - The student's undesired behavior places the student or others at risk of 1) harm or injury and/or 2) exclusion and devaluations (e.g., in the form of multiple suspensions or expulsion).

  - School personnel are considering more intrusive and restrictive procedures and/or a more restrictive placement for the student as a result of increasing degrees of problem behavior.

The Teacher's Guide for Effective Classroom Management: A Trauma-Informed Approach, Third Edition by Tim Knoster and Stephanie Gardner. Copyright © 2024 by Paul H. Brookes Publishing Co., Inc. All rights reserved.

Linking Strategies and Interventions to Hypotheses

A		B	C	Perceived function
Slow triggers (setting events)	Fast triggers (antecedents)	Problem behavior	Consequences	

PREVENTION STRATEGIES

These strategies are identified to address the *A* part of the A-B-C chain (also referred to as the fast and slow triggers, or antecedents and setting events) that is associated with occurrence of the behavior of concern. Look at the triggers (inclusive of those related to trauma) noted in the team's hypothesis statement, and identify things that can be changed instructionally to

- Remove or modify exposure of the student to those triggers
- Block or neutralize the adverse impact of those triggers if they cannot be altered
- Add exposure to desired things (positive triggers) for the student
- Intersperse easy tasks with more difficult tasks in the ebb and flow of instruction

TEACHING ALTERNATIVE SKILLS

These strategies focus on the *A, B,* and *C* parts of the A-B-C chain. There are three types of alternative skills to emphasize:

- Replacement behavior: Look at the identified function (e.g., escape difficult writing tasks, gain teacher attention) in the team's hypothesis statement, and identify an alternative behavior that the student can be instructed to use that serves the same function as the problem behavior. Then, instruct the student to use this replacement behavior to obtain the desired outcome (payoff). Remember, you are not reinforcing the problem behavior; you are simply providing an acceptable way in which the student can obtain the function (e.g., in the case of gaining teacher attention, teach the student to raise hand and provide timely attention when the student raises their hand).

- General skills: Look at the identified skill deficits in your team's hypothesis statement (which most likely would be noted as a slow trigger, such as feeling disconnected/isolated/alone or poor reading skills), and identify general skills to instruct that will help address those skill deficits (e.g., teach social interaction skills, provide instruction to improve reading comprehension skills).

- Coping skills: It is prudent to build in to a behavior support plan the direct instruction of coping skills to enable the student of concern, when feeling frustrated or upset, to use to self-calm. Target simple, physical things that do not require a lot of external materials to facilitate generalization of use of the instructed coping skill(s) to any environment (e.g., deep-breathing skills).

CONSEQUENCE STRATEGIES

- Reinforcement for appropriate behavior: Look specifically at the alternative skills your team has targeted, and look to provide sufficient levels of acknowledgment to the student as they acquire and use these skills over time.

- Responding to problem behavior: Plan to specifically use redirection procedures (e.g., stop, redirect, acknowledge appropriate behavior as previously described in Chapter 9). Be sure to redirect the student, as needed, to use the targeted alternative skills. Then, provide reinforcement for compliance in using the alternative skills. Remember, you are not reinforcing the student's problem behavior. Rather, you are reinforcing (even within the context of your redirection) the student's use of targeted alternative skills (remember to use behavior-specific praise along these same lines).

Keys to Implementing a
Student-Centered Behavior Support Plan

Remember, providing student-centered (individual intensive/tertiary level) behavior support typically requires a team approach.

Be clear about the team's intended outcomes from the onset of design and implementation. In general, successful implementation of a behavior support plan (BSP) should result in 1) reductions in problem behavior, 2) increases in acquisition and use of socially acceptable alternative skills, and 3) meaningful outcomes from the student's and family's perspective.

The behavior support team should meet on a scheduled basis to review performance data and determine needs for changes in the BSP. All plans, even when effective, will require varying forms of modifications over time.

Keep in mind that in most cases, a multicomponent approach is required, and as such, the BSP should reflect prevention strategies, teaching alternative skills and reinforcing both the acquisition and use of alternative skills in tandem with effective and efficient ways in which to redirect problem behavior.

Be sure to address the needs of the members of the team implementing the BSP to best ensure consistent implementation.

There is no set time frame within which to expect desired results from implementing a BSP. The behavior support team should identify what they view as a reasonable time frame to use as a guide as they monitor progress on a regularly scheduled basis.

If reasonable progress is not being realized, start by ensuring that the interventions and supports are being consistently implemented as designed. If the BSP is being implemented consistently, consider modifications to the existent interventions and supports (once again using the hypotheses that summarized the results of the functional behavioral assessment [FBA] as your team's navigational device). Specifically, focus on modifications in preventive, teaching, and consequence interventions and supports. If your team continues to not realize reasonable progress, you may need to expand on the FBA and redevelop hypothesis statements concerning the nature of the student's needs—and in turn develop a new BSP. Consider the integration of the process to design and implement a BSP within the context of a comprehensive wraparound approach with the student and their family if sufficient progress continues to be elusive.

References

Albert, L. (1996). *Cooperative discipline*. AGS Globe.

Archer, A., & Hughes, C. (2011). *Explicit instruction: Effective and efficient teaching*. Guilford Press.

Centers for Disease Control and Prevention (CDC). CDC web-based Injury Statistics Query and Reporting System (WISQARS). *Leading causes of death reports, 1981–2021*. https://webappa.cdc.gov/sasweb/ncipc/leadcause.html

Collaborative for Academic, Social, and Emotional Learning (CASEL). [n.d.]. http://www.casel.org

Cook, C. R., Grady, E. A., Long, A. C., Renshaw, T., Codding, R. S., Fiat, A., & Larson, M. (2017). Evaluating the impact of increasing general education teachers' ratio of positive-to-negative interactions on students' classroom behavior. *Journal of Positive Behavior Interventions, 19*(2), 67–77. https://doi.org/10.1177/1098300716679137

Copeland, W. E., Shanahan, L., Hinesley, J., Chan, R. F., Aberg, K. A., Fairbank, J. A., van den Oord, E. J. C. G., & Costello, J. (2018). Association of childhood trauma exposure with adult psychiatric disorders and functional outcomes. *JAMA Network Open, 1*(7), e184493. https://doi.org/10.1001/jamanetworkopen.2018.4493

Council for Exceptional Children (CEC). (1987). *Academy for effective instruction: Working with mildly handicapped students*. Council for Exceptional Children.

Crone, D. A., Horner, R. H., & Hawken, L. (2004). *Responding to problem behavior in schools: The Behavior Education Program*. Guilford Press.

Desmet, P., & Fokkinga, S. (2020). Beyond Maslow's pyramid: Introducing a typology of thirteen fundamental needs for human-centered design. *Multimodal Technologies and Interaction, 4*(3), 38. https://doi.org/10.3390/mti4030038

Dorado, J. S., Martinez, M., McArthur, L. E., & Leibovitz, T. (2016). Healthy Environments and Response to Trauma in Schools (HEARTS): A whole-school, multi-level, prevention and intervention program for creating trauma-informed, safe and supportive schools. *School Mental Health, 8,* 163–176. https://doi.org/10.1007/s12310-016-9177-0

Felitti, V. J., Anda, R. F., Nordenberg, D., Williamson, D. F., Spitz, A. M., Edwards, V., Koss, M. P., & Marks, J. S. (1998). Relationship of childhood abuse and household dysfunction to many leading causes of death in adults: The Adverse Childhood Experiences (ACE) study. *American Journal of Preventive Medicine, 14*(4), 245–258. https://doi.org/10.1016/S0749-3797(98)00017-8

Gatto, J. T. (2001). *An underground history of American education: A schoolteacher's intimate investigation into the problem of modern schooling*. Oxford Village Press.

Ginott, H. G. (1972). *Teacher and child: A book for parents and teachers*. Macmillan.

Glick, B., & Goldstein, A. P. (1987). Aggression replacement training. *Journal of Counseling & Development, 65*(7), 356–362. https://doi.org/10.1002/j.1556-6676.1987.tb00730.x

Guarino, K., & Chagnon, E. (2018). *Leading trauma-sensitive schools action guide: Trauma-sensitive schools training package*. National Center on Safe Supportive Learning Environments.

Hattie, J. (2015). The applicability of visible learning to higher education. *Scholarship of Teaching and Learning in Psychology, 1*(1), 79–91. https://doi.org/10.1037/stl0000021

Hook, S. (1963). *Education for modern man. A new perspective.* Wipf and Stock.

Hopper, E. K., Bassuk, E. L., & Olivet, J. (2010). Shelter from the storm: Trauma-informed care in homelessness services settings. *The Open Health Services and Policy Journal, 3*(2), 80–100.

Individuals with Disabilities Education Improvement Act (IDEA) of 2004, PL 108-446, 20 U.S.C. §§ 1400 *et seq.*

Jaycox, L. H. (2004). *Cognitive behavioral intervention for trauma in schools.* Sopris West Educational Services.

Johnston, E., D'Andrea Montalbano, P., & Kirkland, D. E. (2017). *Culturally responsive education: A primer for policy and practice.* Metropolitan Center for Research on Equity and the Transformation of Schools, New York University.

Korpershoek, H., Harms, T., de Boer, H., van Kuijk, M., & Doolaard, S. (2016). A meta-analysis of the effects of classroom management strategies and classroom management programs on students' academic, behavioral, emotional, and motivational outcomes. *Review of Educational Research, 86*(3), 643–680. https://doi.org/10.3102/0034654315626799

Lacey, R. E., & Minnis, H. (2020). Practitioner review: Twenty years of research with adverse childhood experience scores–advantages, disadvantages and applications to practice. *Journal of Child Psychology and Psychiatry, 61*(2), 116–130. https://doi.org/10.1111/jcpp.13135

Lane, K. L., Kalberg, J. R., & Menzies, H. M. (2009). *Developing school-wide programs to prevent and manage problem behaviors: A step-by-step approach.* Gilford Press.

Latham, G. I. (1999). *Parenting with love: Making a difference in a day.* P&T Ink.

Loveless, T. (1996). Teacher praise. In H. K. Reavis, M. T. Sweeten, W. R. Jenson, D. P. Morgan, D. J. Andrews, & S. Fister (Eds.), *Best practices: Behavioral and educational strategies for teachers* (pp. 59–63). Sopris West Educational Services.

Maag, J. W. (2001). Rewarded by punishment: Reflections on the disuse of positive reinforcement in schools. *Exceptional Children, 67*(2), 173–186.

MacSuga-Gage, A., & Simonsen, B. (2015). Examining the effects of teacher directed opportunities to respond on student outcomes: A systematic review of the literature. *Education and Treatment of Children, 38*(2), 211–240. https://doi.org/10.1353/etc.2015.0009

Magruder, K. M., Kassam-Adams, N., Thoresen, S., & Olff, M. (2016). Prevention and public health approaches to trauma and traumatic stress: A rationale and a call to action. *European Journal of Psychotraumatology, 7,* 29715. https://doi.org/10.3402/ejpt.v7.29715

Mahoney, J. L., Weissberg, R. P., Greenberg, M. T., Dusenbury, L., Jagers, R. J., Niemi, K., Schlinger, M., Schlund, J., Shriver, T. P., VanAusdal, K., & Yoder, N. (2021). Systemic social and emotional learning: Promoting educational success for all preschool to high school students. *The American Psychologist, 76*(7), 1128–1142. https://doi.org/10.1037/amp0000701

Malloy, J. M., Sundar, V., Hagner, D., Pierias, L., & Viet, T. (2010). The efficacy of the RENEW model: Individualized school-to-career services for youth at risk of school dropout. *Journal of At-Risk Issues, 15*(2), 19–26.

Marzano, R. J., & Marzano, J. S. (2003). The key to classroom management. *Educational Leadership, 61*(1), 6–13.

McIntosh, K., Barnes, A., Eliason, B., & Morris, K. (2014). Using discipline data within SWP-BIS to identify and address disproportionality: A guide for school teams. *OSEP Technical Assistance Center on Positive Behavioral Interventions and Supports.* https://www.pbis.org/resource/using-discipline-data-within-swpbis-to-identify-and-address-disproportionality-a-guide-for-school-teams

Mishra, P., & Koehler, M. J. (2006). Technological pedagogical content knowledge: A new framework for teacher knowledge. *Teachers College Record, 108,* 1017–1054. https://doi.org/10.1111/j.1467-9620.2006.00684.x

Mitchell, B. S., Hirn, R. G., & Lewis, T. J. (2017). Enhancing effective classroom management in schools: Structures for changing teacher behavior. *Teacher Education and Special Education, 40*(2), 140–153. https://doi.org/10.1177/0888406417700961

Mount, B. (1994). Benefits and limitations of Personal Futures Planning. In V. H. Bradley, J. W. Ashbaugh, & B. C. Blaney (Eds.), *Creating individual supports for people with developmental disabilities: A mandate for change at many levels.* Paul H. Brookes Publishing Co.

National Alliance on Mental Illness (NAMI). (2021, October 7). *Young adults with mood disorders often not receiving mental health care, survey finds.* https://www.nami.org/Press-Media/Press-Releases/2021/Young-Adults-with-Mood-Disorders-Often-Not-Receiving-Mental-Health-Care-Survey-Finds

National Institute of Mental Health (NIMH). (2023). *Coping with traumatic events.* https://www.nimh.nih.gov/health/topics/coping-with-traumatic-events

OSEP Technical Assistance Center on Positive Behavioral Interventions and Supports. (2015, October). *Positive Behavioral Interventions and Supports (PBIS) implementation blueprint: Part 1–Foundations and supporting information.* University of Oregon. https://www.pbis.org/resource/pbis-implementation-blueprint

Pace, C., Pettit, S. K., & Barker, K. S. (2020). Best practices in middle level quaranteaching: Strategies, tips and resources amidst COVID-19. *Becoming: Journal of the Georgia Association for Middle Level Education, 31*(1), 2–13. https://doi.org/10.20429/becoming.2020.310102

Pennsylvania Department of Education. (n.d.). *The Pennsylvania Career Ready Skills Continuum.* https://prdeducation.pwpca.pa.gov/K-12/CareerReadyPA/CareerReadySkills/Toolkit/Pages/Continuum.aspx

Pierson, R. (2013, May). *Every kid needs a champion.* [Video]. TED Conferences. https://www.ted.com/talks/rita_pierson_every_kid_needs_a_champion

Quinnett, P. (1995). *QPR: Ask a Question, Save a Life.* The QPR Institute. http:www.qprinstitute.com

Rosen, P., & Lavoie, R. D. (2004). *How difficult can this be? Understanding learning disabilities: Frustration, anxiety, tension, the F.A.T. city workshop* [Full screen version]. PBS Video.

Schaeffer, K. (2022, April 25). *In CDC survey, 37% of U.S. high school students report regular mental health struggles during COVID-19.* Pew Research Center. https://www.pewresearch.org/fact-tank/2022/04/25/in-cdc-survey-37-of-u-s-high-school-students-report-regular-mental-health-struggles-during-covid-19/

Scott, T. M., Alter, P. J., & Hirn, R. G. (2011). An examination of typical classroom context and instruction for students with and without behavioral disorders. *Education and Treatment of Children, 34*(4), 619–641. https://doi.org/10.1353/etc.2011.0039

Simonsen, B., Fairbanks, S., Briesch, A., Myers, D., & Sugai, G. (2008). Evidence-based practices in classroom management: Considerations for research to practice. *Education and Treatment of Children, 31*(3), 351–380. https://doi.org/10.1353/etc.0.0007

Sinclair, M. F., Christenson, S. L., Evelo, D. L., & Hurley, C. M. (1998). Dropout prevention for youth with disabilities: Efficacy of a sustained school engagement procedure. *Exceptional Children, 65*(1), 7–21. https://doi.org/10.1177/001440299806500101

Skinner, B. F. (1953). *Science and human behavior.* Macmillan.

Skinner, E. A., & Belmont, M. J. (1993). Motivation in the classroom: Reciprocal effects of teacher behavior and student engagement across the school year. *Journal of Educational Psychology, 85,* 571–581. https://doi.org/10.1037/0022-0663.85.4.571

Smull, M., & Sanderson, H. (2009). *Essential lifestyle planning for everyone.* The Learning Community – Essential Lifestyle Planning.

Stice, E., Rohde, P., Seeley, J. R., & Gau, J. M. (2008). Brief cognitive-behavioral depression prevention program for high-risk adolescents outperforms two alternative interventions: A randomized efficacy trial. *Journal of Consulting and Clinical Psychology, 76*(4), 595–606. https://doi.org/10.1037/a0012645

Substance Abuse and Mental Health Services Administration (SAMHSA). (2014). *SAMHSA's Concept of trauma and guidance for a trauma-informed approach.* HHS Publication No. (SMA) 14-4884. Rockville, MD.

Substance Abuse and Mental Health Services Administration (SAMHSA) National Child Traumatic Stress Initiative (NCTSI). (2022). *Understanding child trauma.* https://www.samhsa.gov/child-trauma/understanding-child-trauma

Sutherland, K. S., & Wehby, J. H. (2001). Exploring the relationship between increased opportunities to respond to academic requests and the academic and behavioral outcomes of students with EBD: A review. *Remedial and Special Education, 22*(2), 113–121. https://doi.org/10.1177/074193250102200205

Swarbrick, M., & Brown, J. K. (2013). *Mental health first aid USA.* Mental Health Association of Maryland.

The Research and Evaluation Group. (2013). *Findings from the Philadelphia urban ACE survey.* Public Health Management Corporation. https://www.philadelphiaaces.org/philadelphia-ace-survey

U.S. Department of Education, Office of Special Education Programs (OSEP) & Office of Elementary and Secondary Education (OESE) PBIS Center. (2023). *What is PBIS?* https://www.pbis.org/pbis/what-is-pbis

Wolpow, R., Johnson, M. M., Hertel, R., & Kincaid, S. O. (2009). *The heart of learning and teaching: Compassion, resiliency, and academic success.* Washington State Office of Superintendent of Public Instruction Compassionate Schools.

Index

Page numbers followed by *t* and *f* indicate tables and figures, respectively.

You may also be interested in

K–12 teachers: keep these concise how-to guides at your fingertips year after year to help students thrive in virtual learning environments. Created by behavior experts Tim Knoster and Danielle Empson, these practical guides help you:

- Boost positive behavior, engagement, and student wellbeing and in virtual settings
- Take immediate action with teaching tips, proven strategies, and FAQs
- Support students' academic, social-emotional, and behavioral success

Building Relationships With Students and Caregivers to Enhance Learning Through Virtual Instruction

How can you use virtual means of communication to build connections and rapport with students and caregivers? This quick-guide shows how to create healthy relationships in an online classroom and how to identify and connect with students at greater risk for social-emotional and/or academic difficulty.

Enhancing Student Engagement by Virtually Establishing, Teaching, and Reinforcing Desired Behavior

Students in virtual settings need explicit instruction and reinforcement to master behavioral expectations. This guide gives essential tips on the interrelated components of establishing, teaching, and reinforcing desired behavior in an online classroom.

Addressing Undesired Student Behavior During Virtual Instruction

Preventing and addressing undesired behavior is essential—and especially challenging—during online instruction. In this quick-guide, you'll get tips and strategies for preventing undesired behaviors before they start, as well as ways to redirect undesired student behavior in a trauma-informed manner.

Engaging Students in Virtual Instruction Through Opportunities to Respond

Discover how to effectively engage students in your virtual instruction by offering a wider variety of Opportunities to Respond (OTRs). In this guide, you'll learn about the benefits of providing multiple OTRs, the different types and modes for student responses, and how to monitor student engagement virtually.

Order at www.brookespublishing.com | 1-800-638-3775